Copyright 2016 Joie Red

All rights reserved. No part of this publication may be reproduced, stored in a retrieval system or transmitted, in any form or by any means, electronic, mechanical, photocopying, recording or otherwise, without prior written permission of the author, Joie Red. Second edition reprinted 2017.

Note from the Author

This collection of Letters is unofficially, lovingly and anonymously edited. It is the bare bones of my project.

I expect the future team Love Letters to set the grammar straight, and bulk it up – creating tendons, arteries and flesh. I am compelled to distribute it now, believing you, the readers, will breathe life into it. You will give it a beating heart.

Read On

Love Joie

Note #2 from the Author

My aim in 2016 when I launched Love Letters was to spread a little love. The outpouring of love that has rained on me since is simply spectacular! I'm thrilled to share that Team Love Letters is glowing and growing, steadily and tenderly.

j@readred.ca

Joie Red is a fictional character. Any places, events and incidents she shares are either the product of the author's imagination or used in a fictitious manner. Any resemblance readers find to real persons, living or dead, or actual events is purely coincidental.

Call to Readers

These Letters were inspired and written in the spirit of compassion. They are an invitation to readers – empathize and spread love.

2nd Call to Readers

These fifty two Letters highlight how to find love in all the right places, in all the right spaces. Help Joie travel the world and bring love to light.

Dedication

For Tatum – love transcends time and space.

Table of Contents

#1. Home and Native Land 1
#2. Crisscrossed 4
#3. Patchouli Oil................................. 8
#4. Spirit Son 12
#5. Spill the Till 14
#6. Best Barterer 18
#7. Multitudes 22
#8. Bizillionaires.................................. 25
#9. Angel 27
#10. 1990's Style Knight...................................... 29
#11. Valuable 32
#12. Under the Bus 34
#13. Great Man.................................. 37
#14. BFF 40
#15. Same Name 43
#16. Tween Age................................. 45
#17. True Blue Puppy Love..................... 49
#18. Women of Integrity 51
#19. Gone But Not Forgotten 54
#20. Double-Edged Sword Type 60
#21. Shadow of Exhaustion 66
#22. Worldly Wizard 70
#23. Tween Over 73
#24. Yearning & Waiting 77
#25. 3 Heartbeats 81

#26. The Business with the Bunny	85
#27. Belly Button	91
#28. Dam	95
#29. Donut Shop Duo	100
#30. Impromptu Gab Session	105
#31. Sparkler	107
#32. Personal Private Haven	111
#33. Cat & Mouse	115
#34. a-devil-of-a-time	118
#35. Tea in the Shower	121
#36. Tiny Soldier	125
#37. Pendulum	133
#38. Tea Box	138
#39. The Coop	144
#40. Foreign Territory	148
#41. Mask of Static	152
#42. Keep On Knocking	158
#43. Coagulation	162
#44. My Reflection	166
#45. Pearl Drops	170
#46. Spring Walk	175
#47. The Plaque	181
#48. Refuse	185
#49. Glistening Tires	188
#50. Branded	191
#51. Majestic Constellation	197
#52. Subliminal Sausage	200

#1. Home and Native Land

This is a love letter, not a romantic one, none-the-less a love letter.

I am undeniably indebted to you. I was born to you in the summer of your Centennial. It pleases me I became a certified citizen the year you celebrated your 100th birthday. I have been with you now for almost a third of your existence. You are, 'My home and native land.'

My ancestors were some of your Natives, anglers and arborists - they adored you and happily toiled to map out a place for their relations within you. The families multiplied and now live spread across you. I am only an eye witness to a small section of you, yet I revere your beauty.

If not for you, I may have painfully perished shortly after my birth. Also, I had an unusual childhood malady and you freely provided my much-needed medical care. As a youngster I presumed all of humanity received superior medical treatment. I also assumed all people had access to clean water and food and that fresh air lingered everywhere.

Reading was my first love and when the ability to reason developed in me, I was horror-struck to learn of the atrocities committed by the human race. The thought of war torn lands, child soldiers, poverty, oppression and cruelty seemed surreal. I began to realize how fortunate I was to belong to you, and my appreciation has only intensified as I have matured.

It is an honour to be a part of such an exceptional peacekeeping nation.

Yours Always,

Love

Joie Red

#1. Study Questions

Food for Thought

Based only on the information provided in the text:

1. Approximately how old is the Country of reference at the time of this publication?

2. What do you estimate the age of the author to be today?

3. What is the gender of the author?

4. What is the Country of origin of the author?

Matters of the Heart

1. Discuss:
    - (a) female infanticide
    - (b) health care systems within Canada
    - (c) child soldiers
    - (d) equality and freedom at birth.

#2. Crisscrossed

This is a love letter, not a romantic one, none-the-less a love letter.

I was anxiety-ridden meeting you, afraid I would leave feeling frustrated and inferior. Many people before you had tried various teaching techniques with me, and I had hit brick walls in the same areas every time. Even though we only worked together a short while, I have been grateful to you every day for the gift you have given me. More than a decade has passed and the gift keeps giving, making it possible for me to open my life in ways I had not ever imagined.

Your compassionate nature gave you the insight to figure out the type of knot I had in me and how I could unravel it. You interviewed me three times, gathering what you called a 'fact-finding' history on me. With that information in mind you came up with a simple plan - just a suggestion for me to try.

At age 36, as I took up the pen with my left hand, my entire life shifted for the better. Rather than knowing I was smart in some ways, but just plain dull in others, I now considered myself ambidextrous. The more I wrote, the more peaceful I felt. The life-long storm that had brewed within me was smoothly subsiding. I was renewed and rejuvenated.

Although, I had not stuttered all the time, I began to do so less and less. I do not recall the last time I did. My eyes had always flicked multiple times a day, in a blink, roll, blink, sequence of movements, (as if my mind needed a triple take to move on). I cannot express what a relief it is for me to be free of that bothersome tic.

I am delighted that my penmanship has become legible. While in college, if I did not type out my own notes within a few hours, I could not decipher them. Now, I have filled journals and written much correspondence. The letter writing is particularly rewarding to me. I write on blank paper and after a few minutes the words flow out straight and neat, line-by-line. As well, filling out my own forms has considerably boosted my self-confidence.

My reading is not limited to straight text anymore. I take pleasure in newspapers, magazines, and web pages without having to blacken every section save the one on which I need to focus. Steadily and with ease my computer skills have improved. I manoeuvre through internet searches, work on split screens and manage files, happily teaching myself on a need to know basis.

The days of me bumbling numbers appear to be over. It is a very rare happening for me to mix them up. My calendar is orderly, and I have not missed the embarrassment of showing up at the wrong time and day for appointments. Managing my bills is a simple task now as I can read and transpose digits with accuracy.

My fine motor skills are now like those of a different person. Before, when trying to make use of them, I often felt greatly disturbed and would have a panic attack. It was as though my torso was hardened cement and polar magnetic forces twisted me above the waist, clock wise, and below the waist, counter clock wise. It is really liberating to be free of this phenomenon. I am currently able to open and close containers and doors with ease. And I have not stripped the controls on a washing machine since that day. Most amazingly, I have even knitted lovely bags and hats...

The astute way you determined I was a lefty, posing as a righty, was incredible. Thank you for untangling my crisscrossed mystery.

Sincerely,

Joie

#2. Study Questions

Food for Thought

1. Define the term 'Crisscrossed' as the word is used in the title of this Letter.

2. Describe the multiple ways that changing her dominate hand improved Joie's life?

Matters of the Heart

1. What reasons might parents and educators have to force a child to be right-handed?

2. Compile a list of famous left-handed people.

#3. Patchouli Oil

This is a love letter, not a romantic one, none-the-less a love letter.

I know I loved you before we met; you, my true brother, with whom I could talk without words, and with whom I could say anything.

When I first saw you, I was so impressed with the perfect form of your jet-black ringlets that I asked if you spent hours curling your hair before you left your house. Your eyebrows and ringlets bounced with sass as you told me your curly locks were your wife's fault. Our first fit of laughter erupted - it was a deep belly laugh.

My kids and my partner had no problem understanding our special friendship. The children were crazy about you - even your constant teasing did not turn them against you. My spouse respected our friendship, and had a strong affection for you as well. We all relished every smile and chuckle you gave us.

I am so fortunate you brought me to your beautiful family. My love for them has uniquely enriched my life. Converting the power of the laughter we have shared into rocket fuel would enable us to frequent the moon. And the combined energy of our missing you would be potent enough to propel us all on a tour of the universe.

I am beholden to you for many reasons. Our talks were extremely fulfilling. We shared our secrets, all our dreams and regrets. We often butted heads over opposing opinions, which turned out to be reassuring, as I learned the boundaries of sincere friendship were not confining. Our road trips were always entertaining. Even the time we hauled a piano in a treacherous snowstorm, we managed to enjoy ourselves.

We were both prone to strange happenings, a type of physical comedy, like: we had a bizarre way of breaking our bones, we bonked our heads in unexpected places, we awkwardly dropped our belongings into toilets, we were infamous for unintentionally cutting ourselves, and we collided with great hoards of insects. It meant the world to me that I could call you when things of this nature occurred, as your empathy made it impossible not to laugh.

The way we basked in music together was a stronghold of our bond. The concerts and dances where exhilarating, and laying on opposite couches savouring each note of our favourite albums was cathartic. Although I am no fan of that particular four-man band you idolized, I still smile every time I hear them.

Of all the gifts you gave me, teaching me to smudge was one of the best. It is such a healing ritual and I share it with whomever is interested. Last year I performed a welcome smudge, placing my conch inside yours. I burned lavender and sage, to honour our grandchildren.

I wear your belt with the buckle that says 'Great Spirit Guide Me Today.' Doing so feeds my spiritual connection to you. When you came to me in a dream, asking me to join you and your family during your dying days, I went as quickly as I could. It was a tragic and heart wrenching time, yet I felt privileged to be there. With respect, I tried to make myself useful to everyone. It was my privilege to sing for you at the memorial.

One day I will purchase Patchouli Oil...

#3. Study Questions

Food for Thought

1. Define 'smudge.'

2. Discuss the significance of:
   a) the title of this Letter
   b) the quote on the belt buckle
   c) the message in the dream
   d) 'One day I will purchase Patchouli Oil...'

Matters of the Heart

1. Describe a platonic friendship you have witnessed or experienced such as the one brought to light in this Letter.

2. Is there a scent that you love yet find too painful to enjoy?

#4. Spirit Son

This is a love letter, not a romantic one, none-the-less a love letter.

You are the son of my spirit and I carry you with me always. Your soft voice and matter-of-fact way of talking gave me comfort. We laughed silently, cried, rocked on, shared secrets, and made contracts.

The first glimpse of you stole my breath, as you were young and tender, yet you moved like a man who had surrendered after years of battle. You seemed apathetic, but when you smiled, a longing for laughter leaked through the anguish that veiled your eyes.

I knew then great gobs of grief filled your plate and that was long before the murder. He was a tender-hearted person - it was a tragedy. Offering you typical words of consolation would be trite. Yet I want to remind you, you do not have to clear your plate alone - love can help and certainly using your artistry is always a benefit to you and a splendid gift to others.

You, my friend, are like water to a parched palate, necessary and appreciated. I miss you - your soothing voice is like protein to my brain, invigorating and life-giving.

I love you,

Joie

#4. Study Questions

Matters of the Heart

1. Have you met a young person who 'moved like a man who had surrendered after years of battle?'

2. Describe how a smile can tell a story.

3. Whose voice is 'like protein to your brain?'

#5. Spill the Till

This is a love letter, not a romantic one, none-the-less a love letter.

The love you gave me was a vital influence on me becoming a responsible, productive, confident person, with a free sense of humour. You did not give up on me. You believed I could learn and you were extremely patient teaching me.

I cherish the love we had. You gave me a chance when I had burned so many bridges, and found ways to educate me when many others had given up. Thank you for helping me to secure the cornerstones of my life in the proper positions.

You blessed me by teaching me how to work efficiently - it was a confidence builder and a time saver. I often recall you reminding me to save my feet when I could, to not leave a room empty handed. I was so awkward, easily frustrated and nervous, yet you stayed mild mannered and in good humour. Your gentle and enduring nature left me dumbfounded.

Four math teachers and I had given up on me learning mathematical concepts - I just did not have it in me. Yet unbeknownst to me, you opened my mind to that type of thinking. When you dropped all the money out of the till and asked me to help you organize it, I had no idea I was going to learn. By prepping food and organizing the variety of stock, tables and chairs, toilet paper and spices, I gained knowledge. You taught me, a person who was thought to be unreachable.

You irritated me by constantly correcting my manners, and my way of speaking. I thought you were old fashioned and somehow stuck in the 1950's. Yet of course, I taught my children those same manners and ways of speech. For example, we ask, 'May I have some chocolate ice cream please?' There is no saying 'Can I have this?', or 'Can I have that?' Also, when we speak to others we make eye contact and share a genuine smile.

As a teenager, I could not laugh at your antics, but now I keep your spirited sense of humour growing. I reminisce and clown around as well. I would boil with anger when you would tell the customers that as a young child I had accompanied you to the washroom, and boisterously proclaimed, 'Oh I love your fur! Will I get some one day?' I thought you were simply out of your mind the day you peed in your pants while laughing, and it just made you laugh harder. I was mortified when you showed me your toothless, hairless, Halloween costume. I was flabbergasted the time you sternly demanded I meet you in the back kitchen, only to point at a crack in the floor and announce that it was a 'Dirty, dirty, crack!', and that you wanted me to declare a solemn vow right then, that I would always keep my cracks clean. Thank you for the host of hilarious memories.

When you got sick, no one expected it would get the best of you, as you were the epitome of strength, waking at 5:00 a.m. every day and still being on the go well into the evening. I could bring you to only one of your chemo treatments and for many years, I felt I had deeply disappointed you. In retrospect, I am certain you understood my immature heart did not have the ability to get off the top of the erupting volcano it was on.

I lacked the maturity to move myself aside and be there for you.

You were a magnificent person, who worked wonders with so many of us. Although it has been many years since you died, we speak of you often, in the spirit of love and laughter.

You are dearly missed.

Love Joie

#5. Study Questions

Food for Thought

1. Why do you think Joie was able to successfully learn skills from the woman in this Letter which she had previously not been able to learn?

2. What are the four main styles of learning? What style was the woman using with Joie when she purposely dropped the contents of the till?

Matters of the Heart

1. When has your heart been stuck on the top of an erupting volcano?

2. What are the cornerstones of your life and who helped you place them in position?

#6. Best Barterer

This is a love letter, not a romantic one, none-the-less a love letter.

You are one of my idols. Your tender touch, the adoring way you looked at me, and the doting way you spoke to me, made me feel extraordinary. You enriched my life, and gave me much to look forward to - you rocked my world! I looked super happy and at ease in all of our pictures together. I basked in your touch. Thank you for all the cuddles, laughter, and attention. I was glad to be alive when you were with me.

I have never met anyone who could hold a candle to you, as you had such an extensive range of character traits. You loved being with people and could talk to anyone - street people, priests, politicians and gangsters. You definitely had the gift of gab.

Even at the famous discount store they knew you were one of the best barterers, always getting a 15 to 20% discount. It was exciting to watch you in action, making deals, whether it was at the wholesaler's, a second hand shop, a bar, or a swanky hotel - you acquired price cuts.

The gift of music was one of yours. Hearing you sing and bang those spoons blew my mind. When I was old enough, and we went out together, I was proud to tell the band to relinquish the mike to you - what a dancer you were, you moved with complete abandon. Thank you for showing me a woman can be: strong, beautiful, gifted, smart, funny, compassionate, sexual, resourceful, wise, entertaining, and independent.

Even though it took me years to emulate many of your ways (and I am still working on it), I was empowered by your spirit of forgiveness, your spunk for life, the faith that kept you going, and the way you helped others. I do not hold a grudge or judge people harshly. Like you, I will not allow myself to rust - I get up and out, keeping my body and mind moving. Although my faith is different from yours, it is the driving force of my life, and I help others whenever I can.

When you needed palliative care, they asked me to think about what I would like of yours; I could have anything. In my devastation, I did not think I wanted anything of yours, as I expected you to recover. Eventually I did ask for one of the watches I was fond of as a child, and the blanket we had cuddled under together.

In my grief, I do not recall bringing the blanket into my room, but I know I kept it sealed in there. At times I would take it out to allow your scent to linger through the room; the aroma would put me at ease, a comforter providing comfort. When the scent was no longer noticeable, I used the blanket on my bed until it was threadbare - then I cut it into squares to add to a family quilt.

On the way to your funeral, I witnessed a heart stirring tribute to you. I felt it before I saw it - a powerful peaceful hush cascaded over your old block drowning out the city sounds. Hearing the hush I knew something mystical was transpiring. A throng of people stood stately, with their heads bowed and their backs against the wall of that grand Church on your old corner.

I began to weep, for I knew that those folks wrapped around the mission walls would sincerely miss you.

The tears warmed my skirt as they fell, and my mind flooded with the images of you, being with those so-called rough and tumble-type people. I recalled you chatting with them, passing them money, flowers, clothes and coffee. My tears turned cold, as I silently bawled, not wanting to believe you were gone.

Occasionally I still pick up the phone intending to call you. At first, the number was in my speed dial and for a long time I was shocked when a recording came on saying the number was out of service. Then after a time, to my disbelief, a stranger answered - I threw away the phone. A few years ago, I felt I had let you down when I failed to remember the number. After a time of crying, I realized although I may have forgotten the number, I honour your memory every day. Everyone in my life knows how remarkable you were and I made sure my children felt the love you gave me.

Thank you for adoring me,

Love Joie

#6. Study Questions

Food for Thought

1. What was the nature of the relationship between Joie and the 'Best Barterer?'

2. What play on words is the statement 'a comforter providing comfort?'

Matters of the Heart

1. How do you relate to the grief expressed in this Letter?

2. At what points in this Letter do you identify Joie experiencing denial in her grief? Share similar experiences.

#7. Multitudes

This is a love letter, not a romantic one, none-the-less a love letter.

As one of the multitude I long for you to know you are not alone. What happened then was wrong, and you are not to blame. I want you to dispose of the wet net that trapped you - smother it with compassion. As it vaporizes you will gain confidence, and care for yourself better. Hearts and souls renew; rejuvenation can be ours.

I could not write you then as I did not know you existed. If writing to him was not against one of the rules at age 14 I would have written:

> You are the best looking man ever! I take pride in protecting our secret relationship Cause I know our special friendship is a Once In A Life Time Chance! No one could be more loyal to you than ME Cause I know you'd literally drop dead without me! Don't worry I will always be here for you! Don't worry I'm not mad Cause lately it hurts real bad. I know a lot had to change after I was raped. I am one lucky lady having the chance to learn stuff as soon as my buds started budding. Thank you for seeing my rare maturity! You know I'm no baby, really I'm more like a 30 year old woman than a young girl.
>
> Your Friend FOREVER

I would not have told him that I secretly despised him and I wished the police would get him. Or that I fantasized about someone killing him. I was plagued with guilt when I thought this way because he loved me and taught me so much - I knew I should be grateful for all he did.

Enough about him, as I mentioned, this letter is for you. We are countless and have existed in both genders, at all ages, always. Please find solace in this rather than becoming embittered.

This absurd dynamic will not cease, yet I do believe we can combat it. We can hobble it, weaken its vile effects and shrink its venue. A lone snowflake with its originality and beauty has little influence on its setting, yet together scores of them can change an entire landscape.

This is my love letter to all those who were trapped when they were young or vulnerable. Let us change the landscape.

Take Care,

Love Joie

#7. Study Questions

Food for Thought

1. Define paedophilia.

2. Who are the subjects of this Letter?

3. At what age of remembrances, perspective and experience did Joie write the letter within this Letter?

4. Paraphrase the first and second-last paragraphs of this Letter.

Matters of the Heart

1. Define victim.

2. If a young person is victimized, when is it reasonable to expect them to free themselves of a victim mentality?

3. Write your own Letter to the man Joie wrote to within this Letter.

#8. Bizillionaires

This is a love letter, not a romantic one, none-the-less a love letter.

Thank you both for coming to stay with me as you did. Your love for each other was a delight to me. When you acquired your own place, it was sweet that you willingly took the cat we could not care for and gave her a great home. Your youthful spirits lightened mine. I enjoyed your openness and the countless remarkable conversations the three of us shared. You respected each other with such a natural grace; no one could rightfully call your relationship puppy love.

You demonstrated respect beyond your years. Even through life's frustrations you found a way to laugh and what contagious laughter it was. I have a picture of the two of you sharing a chair, it was a typical pose, the two of you touching yet not distasteful.

I smile when I think of your bright sets of eyes, as you explained how neat it was her left breast was quite larger than her right and even if you were bizillionaires you would not change them. I wonder how both of you are. I hope as life unfolds you are each able to continue to find laughter and love in everyday.

Love Joie

#8. Study Questions

Food for Thought

1. Discuss plastic surgery being sure to consider:
   - (a) breast implants
   - (b) breast lifts
   - (c) breast augmentations
   - (d) breast reductions.

Matters of the Heart

1. When have you met a young couple who seemed to be respectful beyond their years? Describe why and what character traits and behaviours they demonstrated that make you feel this way.

#9. Angel

This is a love letter, not a romantic one, none-the-less a love letter.

How fortunate I was to be your *pet*. You showed me what a virtuous woman was, gave me a platform to reach for. Knowing you believed I would do well made me courageous. Thank you for all your dedication and patience. I cherish the memories of the many hugs and kisses you gave me and I loved hearing you boast to your friends about me.

I am amazed at all the changes you witnessed in your life, yet you stayed true to your beliefs. You were such an honourable woman. You treasured your faith and even upon your deathbed you were unafraid. The only thing that bothered you was we would be sad, and it hurt you to think of us crying.

You did a great deal for me, taking me to live with you, believing in me, constantly praying for me, and eventually letting me fall. I am forever grateful for all you did. I was ashamed to have disappointed you and fortunate you were able to witness me getting on the right track.

When you stayed with me for those months, I could not have been more pleased. Moreover, you enjoyed your stay! How delighted I was. At the time, you referred to me as one of your Angels! How could that be, you were the most Angelic person I have ever known?

Thank you for believing in me.

Love Joie

#9. Study Questions

Matters of the Heart

1. In your opinion what makes a woman virtuous and honourable?

2. Joie referred to the subject of the Letter as 'the most Angelic person' she had ever known. Who is the most Angelic person you have ever known? And why?

#10. 1990's-Style Knight

This is a love letter, not a romantic one, none-the-less a love letter.

You do give the gift of laughter to those around you which moved me to tears many times.

Your spunk is what I relate to the most, it sparkled out of your dark eyes like a welder's arc. Our affection for each other was obvious. Your mother said our connection made sense as it takes one ballsy person to know one. You were so young and sturdy then - it seemed as though a car could have run you over and you would have simply got up and walked away.

I recall how wide-eyed you were watching me cry as you played that ballad of family heartbreak for me. Thank you for introducing me to that female pop star. I take great pleasure in all her music now.

I cherish the delicious talks we had, the many memorable meals we shared and all the fun-filled outings we went on. You are one of the few people who stuck up for me, my personal valiant 1990's-style Knight. I appreciated you confiding in me. It was easy for me to listen to you. It was mad-fun sharing the details of our latest reads together – I do hope you keep on reading. I found it heart warming and sad when you did not want me checking on you so much anymore.

As outlandish as it may seem, I found your obstinate manner enticing. You yelled until you were hoarse, dressed to please only yourself and harassed the girls into tears a few times a week.

Your real rebellious nature revealed itself boldly the day of the unmerited shake-down. You did not quiver or cry when the doors were kicked in by a crew of gigantic growling police officers and when one of the giants pointed a rifle at you and barked 'Put down your phone!' you met his gaze and asked in a matter-of-fact-way 'Can I not finish my phone call?'

The intensity of your spirit and character denotes that of a fearless leader. It is my privilege to have spent a few years with you. I sit delighted in my seat on the sidelines of your life.

Go-get-um,

Love Joie

#10. Study Questions

Food for Thought

1. What is in the text of this Letter that lets readers know:
   (a) why Joie and the subject could be called kindred spirits?
   (b) the age difference between Joie and the subject?

Matters of the Heart

1. Discuss the necessity of policing including:
   (a) search and seizure
   (b) use of force
   (c) raiding.

2. Define and discuss stereotyping.

3. Have you ever experienced what you consider to be an unmerited shake down?

#11. Valuable

This is a love letter, not a romantic one, none-the-less a love letter.

Meeting you in my first year of high school was one of the best things that had ever happened to me. You are a rarity within your profession, a teacher who had a wonderful, deep and lasting impact on my life. Your instruction and encouragement gave my life meaning, as well as a compelling reason to attend school.

The first day of class, you directed us all to begin singing, only moments later to stop us, to ask me to sing solo. I let out a few bars, and quickly you invited me down to stand next to your piano and sing the classic of all classic rock ballads. That moment was defining and magical for me. Discovering I had the ability to make people smile transformed me. I traded in my status as a freak for that of a valuable commodity.

I took much more than the singing from your teaching; I realized I was able to do well in school, to persevere in all things sensible and that I was valuable. Thank you for choosing to share your gift of music with me.

Warmest Regards,

Joie

#11. Study Questions

Food for Thought

1. Aside from the gift of music what did Joie gain from this particular teacher?

2. What teacher had a 'deep and lasting impact' on your life? Describe.

Matters of the Heart

1. Identify and discuss the pro's and con's of subcultures within school systems.

2. What subculture or subcultures do you identify within:
   (a) the world
   (b) your country
   (c) your city
   (d) your place of work?

#12. Under the Bus

This is a love letter, not a romantic one, none-the-less a love letter.

I knew something was amiss when a goose-bump-like sensation raced over me, and that familiar fight or flight feeling made me queasy. I looked around and found a city bus had stopped at an undesignated area. The passengers and driver appeared dazed and stiff like mannequins – the scene was sinister and senseless, as if from a science-fiction movie.

As I moved closer to the bus, the scent of alcohol seeping out the pores of one's skin led me to a man tucked under the middle wheel-well of the bus. I swiftly approached him to find he was hugging the tires, mumbling repeatedly 'I'll never never never let go.'

He was petite and covered in layers of grime that matched the stench of him. A bottle of booze was stuck so extremely tight in his left back pocket, I knew it took a unique expertise to get it to fit in that way, and he would have to pull his pants down to get it out.

I knelt and asked him if he could use a hand, and would he let me help him to get out from under the bus. He rolled over and limply reached out to me. I assisted him to his feet, away from the bus.

As the bus swiftly sped off I speculated as to what would happen next. Would he become belligerent? Would we talk a while? When did he last draw a sober breath? Would he physically lash out at me? Would we share a meal? When did this man last feel a tender embrace? Would he ever sober up? Would we see each other after today? When did he last work? I envisioned him cleaned up, healthy and restored.

I asked him where he needed to be and through slow, slurred speech he claimed he needed to come home with me, as I was his angel. I lead him to a stoop at the plaza where we sat together silently for a few moments.

I gently pleaded with him to attend the detox or hospital, explaining the folks there could help him to get on his feet. He answered me by stiffly and abruptly turning his body away, cranking his neck up to the sky and sending me serious screw-off vibes. I sat with him for a few more moments. As I got up to walk away I lightly squeezed his shoulder, and said 'Stay out from under the buses.'

As I left him I gained a keen awareness of the beauties of the day. I rejoiced in the inhalation of the fresh crisp fall air, soaking in the brilliance of the rust-red and multi-yellow coloured leaves. I knew my mentors would be pleased with me for giving a hand to a man under a bus...

Keep on rolling,

Love Joie

#12. Study Questions

Food for Thought

1. How do you define alcoholism?

2. What is your initial reaction to the physical description of the man and the scene where Joie found him?

Matters of the Heart

1. Paragraph five lists some questions Joie asked herself regarding the man she encountered. Write your own paragraph of questions about the man in this Letter.

#13. Great Man

This is a love letter, not a romantic one, none-the-less a love letter.

You are one of the few great men in my life. Thank you for the way you have loved me through the years.

I want you to know how much I appreciate and treasure all the time we have shared together.

The day we met you were saddled with a scared mixed-up girl, who had just let go of dangling on the fringes of society. Your majestic stature shook me, yet you carried yourself with such grace and eloquence - I was intrigued. The patience and tolerance you have bestowed upon me for all these years is incredible. As I struggled to find my place in life, you were there, setting a first-rate example.

You became a confidant to me, guiding me through life. It meant a great deal to me knowing you were in my corner. How can I express my gratitude for everything you have given me and my loved ones? The way you welcomed my Dad and later the children was amazing. You have helped us all so much along the way.

You were the one there, camera in hand, capturing memories of all my family's milestones. The kids were very fortunate to grow up sharing holidays with you. Through the passing of their formative years, they knew you loved them. Of course children enjoy tangible presents, yet it is the memories of *fun* they value the most: swimming, feeding the ducks, sharing meals, road trips, parties, laughing, seeing you in your uniform, cleaning cars, garage sailing, picnics, exploring the outdoors, attending concerts, watching you shave...

Words fail to convey the meaningful impact your positive masculine influence had on them during their childhoods.

I was thrilled with the yearly solo trip you would make to spend a few nights with me. It was so thoughtful of you to fill those days helping me around our home. They were special visits, filled with belly laughs, private talks, problem solving, and lovely dinners. I felt so proud and honoured every year when you spent private time with me.

As sure as time passes, circumstances change. Although the grand scheme is beyond me, I do not begrudge this being so. Nevertheless, when the situation in your life changed leaving you absent from mine, I bitterly missed you but thankfully love has a way of lingering.

During the *shock* period of Mom passing you were my rock. It must have been very difficult for you, yet you were there for me. I was able to keep one foot in front of the other, maintain a lady-like composure, and come through the ordeal stronger because you let me lean on you. When I told you what I experienced in her last moments you validated me as no one ever has. I do not think I would have been able to recover without the wisdom you shared and the comfort you gave me.

Thank you,

Love Joie

#13. Study Questions

Food for Thought

1. What do you feel was the nature of the relationship between Joie and the 'Great Man?' Describe a similar relationship you have experienced or witnessed.

2. What do you feel was the nature of the relationship between the children mentioned and the 'Great Man?'

3. Make a list of character traits of the 'Great Man.'

4. What is revealed about the physical appearance of the 'Great Man?'

Matters of the Heart

1. What is your definition of family?

Considering:
(a) the relevance and necessity of blood ties in forming family
(b) what obligations family members have to each other.

#14. BFF

This is a love letter, not a romantic one, none-the-less a love letter.

I had hopped around that College for almost two weeks before I met you. I was performing my five-part get through the door routine when you called out to me. The routine involved firstly holding myself steady on the crutches, then giving a swift right kick to the door. Next, was a jump with a half twist to the left. Fourthly I had to secure my butt in position to hold the door open and then finally I could vault through.

I was ready to vault when I heard you call out, asking if you could get the door for me. I had not remembered hearing a sweeter voice or kinder words and with great sincerity, I replied by telling you I thought I loved you. Then I caught sight of you and I knew you were easy to love, as an aura of compassion and optimism surrounded you.

I found you to be an extremely attractive young woman and even though you were 19, you could have passed for a 13 year old. You intrigued me. Your face was fantastically fresh, and your unique eyes emitted a stress-free energy. We became walking partners. It was such a relief for me to have you with me opening the doors. Decades have rolled by since, and your friendship has opened many doors for me. I had not expected to have a Best Friend Forever, and I treasure every moment we share.

We had such polar personalities then; me the skeptic, you the eternal optimist, me intense, you so easy going, me sleeping little, you loving to sleep in. We used to joke that combined we made one strong, balanced and level headed woman. We were a dynamic team, helping each other through those challenging College days. I found the program very satisfying, yet our friendship was the lasting and greatest reward I took from my college experience.

I am eight years older than you - it seemed a great span then, me having my kids and you still living at home. Fortunately, we did not let the differences in our stages of life hold us back. A smart choice, for now my children look up to you and your child trusts me. Thank you for sharing that love with me. Your child has been an absolute joy to me, as a newborn and straight on through to now, the teenager.

Life has unfolded letting loose many wondrous and trying situations for each of us. Through it all our friendship keeps broadening. You prefer to share your troubles little, and only after they have passed, whereas I hit the phone to you almost immediately. You are a nighthawk I wake early now, otherwise our differences are minor. We have shared and enmeshed our traits, both of us becoming less extreme in our ways - life is not so clear-cut anymore.

These days the Colleges have electric doors, a simple push and presto they open. Fortunately for me you made my way accessible. When I am with you, the spinning top in me always slows down a bit - you make everything easier for me.

Your love is radiance in my darkness, and a sun visor in my blind spots.

Love Your BFF Always,

Joie

#14. Study Questions

Food for Thought

1. Discuss
   (a)　accessibility
   (b)　accommodation
   (c)　disability awareness

Matters of the Heart

1. Have you met someone who had an 'aura of compassion and optimism?' Please elaborate.

2. How has the love of a friend provided 'radiance in your darkness and a sun visor in your blind spots?'

#15. Same Name

This is a love letter, not a romantic one, none-the-less a love letter.

My love for you is uncanny. It must have begun long before we arrived on earth. Our names are the same, we are both of small physical stature, yet our voices are strong and clear. I love you for the amazing example you have shown me, for all the details and big stuff in life you outlined for me.

Thank you for loving me and for: giving me shoes to wear when my feet were dirty and bare, making me wear a bra, teaching me to pray, to walk upright and how to walk in heels, to us profanity only when acceptable, to bite my tongue instead of reacting.

You blessed me by teaching me how to knit, requiring me to speak softly, telling me over and over I am worthy, apologizing as necessary and clearing the way for me to *own up*. You made life better for all of us by helping me to parent, to be a healthy partner and a polite daughter.

I am grateful to you for letting me know it is healthy for most people to flirt, that I can infect those around me with a smile and for not giving up on me as I *stand up* and morph into a lady.

I treasure the many clothes, bags, music boxes, mugs, furniture, slippers, knick-knacks, photos, jewellery, pictures and other tangible mementoes you have given me. They are all a part of my home and your love life lessons are a part of my personality.

Over and Out For Now

Love Joie

#15. Study Questions

Food for Thought

1. What did you learn about Joie's physicality in this Letter?

2. Speculate as to the longevity and nature of the relationship Joie has with the subject of this Letter?

Matters of the Heart

1. Literally or figuratively who has given you shoes when your feet were dirty and bare? Share the circumstances and the nature of the relationship you have with this person.

2. Do you have items in your home that are of sentimental value to you? If so what are they and how did you acquire them?

#16. Tween Age

This is a love letter, for you, my true and best friend.

The day I first saw you was a crisp-aired autumn day, in the late seventies. I had not wanted to meet you and had strongly protested. I did not need a boyfriend. Our mutual red-headed friend was determined I would be your girl. He relentlessly insisted, constantly claiming the cool city boy and I would be a perfect match. I gave in, and agreed to go as long as we met in a dark place. It was a tween-aged blind date.

I had planned for us to get together in the old leather factory, so I was horror-struck as you approached us on the street. I did not want you to see me in broad daylight! I dug in my heels and begged our friend not to make me go. He held me under my arms and pulled me along. I kicked and squirmed out of his grasp and stole a glance at you. Your hair captivated me - that loose afro looked to me like a magical, mysterious helmet. I could see you had a bum right arm. It was shorter than the left and it stuck out and upwards at the elbow, bringing to mind a bird with a busted wing. This visible uniqueness set me at ease - maybe I did not have to be doll-like beautiful to be a genuine girlfriend.

My heart pumped to a brand new beat as we approached each other. You were not much bigger than me, and I found you to be *sooooo cute*. As we drew near, I moved away, pushing our friend in between us. We began walking together. I experienced a new kind of buzz when I caught you checking me out with your peripheral vision. It made my body quiver in an electrifying way - it was a frightening and foreign sensation. I was apprehensive to make eye contact with you, fearing I might vanish into your hazel eyes.

We had not walked far when our friend dashed from between us and shoved me against you. The scent I inhaled from your neck set off a colossal change in me. Never mind love at first sight - this was love at first sniff. Both my grandmothers and their homes had a soothing, comforting smell yet no scent had affected me like yours. The fine hairs on my arms and the back of my neck surged up and every cell of my skin was stirring. I felt giddy - one whiff of you turned me, the infamous tomboy, into a genuine love-struck girl.

Our introduction had gone well, our friend was awfully pleased. I had an *Old Man* and you had an *Old Lady*, terms of endearment we still use today.

During the next several years we clung together, passing endless hours walking and talking. Needing to touch each other as often as possible, we habitually held hands. Often times I sat on your shoulders - you tell folks I gave you your broad shoulders. We would walk as one, me tucked under your arm, stepping in perfect unison. You were so kind and gentle I knew I was the luckiest in love and I would have the best husband in the world.

We perfected the art of kissing - you were always finding private spots for us to be together. The concrete dock was my favourite place. Plunging into the water and popping up underneath in the proper spot guaranteed we could suspend from our forearms with headroom to spare. That was our highly classified kissing space, the water was clear and clean then. We were oblivious to everyone who was walking above us. We pressed our lips together endlessly, paying no heed when they went numb.

We were extremely proud of each other and grew closer every day. Part of our plan was to have four children, whom we would never hit because we were going to be gentle parents...

Love Always,

Your Joie

#16. Study Questions

Food for Thought

1. What age bracket was Joie in when this Letter took place?

2. The scent of Joie's soon to be boyfriend caused a chemical reaction within her body which she had never experienced before.
   (a) Why did his scent affect her differently than any other person she had met?
   (b) Name and define this chemical reaction between human beings?

3. Discuss the purpose and function of the olfactory centre in human beings.

Matters of the Heart

1. Recall when you were first affected by someone's gaze the way Joie was by her blind-date. Please recount your experience.

2. If you had an eleven year-old granddaughter what would you want her to understand about her sensual and sexual self?

#17. True Blue Puppy Love

This is a love letter, not a romantic one, none-the-less a love letter.

I was madly in love with you, true blue puppy love! As much as a nine-year-old-girl could be in love, I was with you. I found the pale green polyester suit you wore when we met stunning, and even more beautiful were your sheer blue eyes. I saw an entirely new world in them that day, a strange but magnetically inviting way of being. You bent to shake my hand and as you spoke, the sound of your voice started to melt something in me; a part of me I was too young to know was frozen. From that day on, the look of your eyes and the sound of your voice has reassured and encouraged me. My heart gushes with gratitude for what you did, for so many others and for me.

You were a fine man, a student of spiritual ways with a love for: laughter, storytelling, dance, family, work and friendship. Not many trailblazers and torchbearers have a kind-hearted way of leading others as you did. Your family and all of us will miss you every day.

You will always be my first love. Thank you for igniting the spark in my despair and fanning its flame. You gave me hope.

Love you...

Joie

#17. Study Questions

Matters of the Heart

1. Have you seen a strange but magnetically inviting way of being in another person? Describe what you saw in that person.

2. Has the sound of someone's voice started to melt something in you that you didn't even know was frozen? Write a thank you note to the person.

3. Has someone ignited a spark in your despair and helped you to fan its flame? Discuss the circumstances.

#18. Women of Integrity

This is a love letter, not a romantic one, none-the-less a love letter.

I love you both very much. You are a delight to be near and I will be forever grateful for what you did for me. I recall how lively you were and you looked especially fresh. There was a genuine oomph behind all your gestures. Your eyes secreted serenity and although it seemed completely out of my reach, I longed to possess it. It is now 29 years later and you are still brimming over with life; thankfully I share in that life. I wake looking forward to each day and try to be a woman of integrity, a tribute to you both.

I was 17 and very sick, close to death when you took an interest in me. The whites of my eyes were yellow, my pancreas visibly swollen, and my brain wet. There was no way to know if I could improve, yet you encouraged me, brought me to the treatment centre and insisted that they keep me. Unbeknownst to me, you injected love into my spirit that day. That love simmered in me and as I slowly improve it multiplies.

I know it did not seem like I could hear your suggestions then but believe me I was listening. As my body healed and my brain began to replenish I remembered your advice. I am still working on enacting healthy habits and have had set backs, but wow, I am 46 and have a grandchild.

I am appreciative of all you have taught the others and me. Thanks to both of you I know I am not alone - I am free just to be me; forgiveness is *key*.

With Everlasting Love,

Joie

#18. Study Questions

Food for Thought

1. Name and define the medical term for wet brain.

2. Why are heavy drinkers at risk of developing wet brain?

3. Define juvenile alcoholism/addiction.

4. Research rates of alcoholism/addiction occurring in youth in your area.

Matters of the Heart

1. Have you ever realized that unbeknownst to you, someone injected love into your spirit? Please elaborate.

2. What do 'eyes that secrete serenity' look like?

#19. Gone But Not Forgotten

This is a love letter, not a romantic one, none-the-less a love letter.

The first time I went to your grave I laid down right on top of it, communing with the marrow of you that remained. Inwardly I asked you to forgive me for not going sooner and for suppressing my memories. As I willed our spirits to greet, a bundle of emotions overtook me. The tears I had held in for fourteen years began to drop, but your presence prevailed. It was the first time since your death I really allowed myself to be with you, to remember you as you were, as we were together, and to ponder all that you had missed by passing so young. I was comfortable and pleased to be lying there. I had a sense of security just as if you were watching my back.

After that, I was able to let my memories flow and frequented the north end to your gravesite, not our part of town, but to my relief not on snob hill. I know how we felt about snob hill.

Gone But Not Forgotten

I sit by your grave
And try to be brave
Thinking of all you gave

You my dear friend are gone yet never forgotten
Though your flesh has crumbled like worn cotton
Your fiery ways to me are not misbegotten

You live on through me and my memories
I tell of you clearly, it's like growing trees
Everyone who hears the words clearly sees

I sit by your grave
And try to be brave
Thinking of all you gave

How I loved you from the day we met
And my feelings for you haven't eased up yet
Our hearts in the cast where they were set

I am coupled with the one of your choice
Thank you so, as he has the sweetest voice
Together we make daily reasons to rejoice

I sit by your grave
And try to be brave
Thinking of all you gave

I miss you so and try not to be mad
For all the beauty that I have had
But you got robbed ever-so-bad

I want to talk to you on your cell phone
And tell you that *they* can make a clone
But I sit where your name is on a stone

I sit by your grave
And try to be brave
Thinking of all you gave

When I first met you I noticed the bounce in your step was unique. I liked your red wavy shoulder length hair and your cool blue-grey eyes. The way your fingers rounded at the ends and your knuckles bulged was distinct. What intrigued me the most though, were the billions of freckles that covered you. They each had a life force of their own and only a hint of creamy white skin shone through. You were not much bigger than I was, yet your voice had a strong masculine tone. It exuded a confidence that commanded respect.

Within an hour of meeting we had formed a super-glue-type strong bond. I was ecstatic not to be a solo act anymore and proud you were my first *partner*. My plight would have been much worse if you had not watched out for me and taught me the ropes. Even our fights, (and we had some knock down drag-um-out ones) helped me cope with what was to come. Thank you for being my *partner* and for having my back. I want you to know my love for you is as tight as ever.

There are so many things I long to tell you, I am not sure where to begin. My *Old Man* is the one you picked for me. What a great choice he was, we are a powerful couple. I have been a straight-ass most of my life. Yes I am a bona fide square. It was either that or death. I just live, not on one side or the other - I live a simple life that is peaceful. My friend, we have a grandchild. You would be amazed watching the three of us together, the little one and us, Nanna and Papa.

Technology has changed in leaps and bounds since we saw that Super Star guy talking on a car phone in a limo. My computer is not much bigger than that phone was. I have a music player which holds 10,000 songs, and is the size of a square fifty cent piece. What a change from the ghetto blaster we had! We used to call each other from one payphone to another. Now people text and video call - the world does not wait anymore. There are cameras recording almost everywhere, even our main drag is under video surveillance. Oh, how I would love to reminisce face-to-face with you and compare the old days to now.

My Dad was the one who told me you had died. When I saw him I knew there had been a tragedy by the twisted expression on his face. The skin on his face hung unnaturally, bringing to mind a full-length silk gown having gone through an unbalanced spin cycle. When I asked him what happened, he choked out that he had something terrible to tell me, and I snapped at him to spit it out. When he began rocking side-to-side and blubbering 'God why him, God I loved that kid.' My chest visibly rattled like a rumbling rocket preparing to launch. He looked at me through his swollen eyes and pleadingly mumbled, 'Remember, remember? How he would put his mouth on the window, remember, remember?'

I knew my Dad was referring to you, as you had trademarked the-mouth-on the-window-thing as your departing gesture. You fixed your mouth wide open on the window, blew as much air into your cheeks as you could, and then let your tongue just go crazy on the glass. A picture perfect reel of you doing your window-thing ran in slow motion through me, stilling me. I was in a trance. The trance was infiltrated by the clear cohesive faint murmur of my inner voice - somehow my freckled friend may have died.

The noise of my Dad's bawling sent a piercing pain shooting under my ribs. I hollered at him, stating I did not remember much about you, but I did remember I was pregnant and he was upsetting me. I retorted I needed him to shut up and get out. He hounded me, demanding I attend your funeral with him. Only when I consented to accompany him to one of the viewings and hug your mother did he agree to leave.

When he took me to the funeral home a few days later, he was weeping, yet his tears had no affect on me. It was as though I hovered on an invisible escalator inside the building into the doorway of the room. I hugged the woman my Dad instructed me to but refused to mimic him any further. I was limp in the archway akin to a lightly held marionette; he waited in line for the coffin. I saw him kneel on the pad in front of the burial box and as he reached inside the coffin, an icy shiver descended upon me.

It pounded the crown of my head, gushing down to the tips of my toes, forcefully shaking me. It was as if I was scrambling in ballet slippers on an ice rink. I placed my palms flat against the wall to brace myself. My Dad stood and I saw his body unnaturally contorting - he was silently howling.

I had an overwhelming urge to flee before he came back towards me. As I attempted to take my hands off the wall, your coffin came into my view.

For a spilt-second I saw what resembled a wax figure of you. Even from that distance I could tell your freckles had altered. They were flat and dull. They were no longer a billion independent forces. Rather they resembled an image of a water-soiled oil painting, blurry and barely recognizable.

Abruptly my balance returned and I walked out treading heavily, holding myself up with a silent yet deep footing. The movement gave me clarity of mind. I thought it terribly sad that your freckles had melted, and I questioned, why I had not been there to defend you...

Love Joie,

Just a Stupid Girl

#19. Study Questions

Food for Thought

1. Define the stages of grief.

2. Note where you think each stage applies to Joie in this Letter and track the pattern and duration of her stages of grief. What are some of the factors that influenced her grief journey?

3. Joie refers to the deceased person as her '*partner*' noting they had a 'super-glue-type strong bond.' Discuss the dynamics of this relationship.

Matters of the Heart

1. Joie shared her 'trance was infiltrated by the clear cohesive faint murmur of her inner voice' telling her 'somehow her freckled friend may have died.' Share instances when your inner voice has whispered to you.

2. What is your experience with survivor's guilt?

#20. Double-Edged Sword Type

This is a love letter, not a romantic one, none-the-less a love letter.

Until then I had taken you for granted but since that moment my thoughts of you are polar; I find you insufferable, or I appreciate the hell out of you.

You repulsed me that day - you were so twisted and unnatural looking. I began my fear-filled relationship with you when I heard the popping and tearing you screamed out. Even through the shock, I knew I was going to find out just how much I depended on you.

As they pulled off my boot I was deeply disgusted seeing you torn open just as trees hit by a tornado. The remnants were jagged and splintery. My vision blurred and I woke many hours later moaning in pain. It was an unimaginable burning sensation, as though a white-hot steel rod were pushing up through my heel. I passed the next several weeks alternating between the fiery pain and a place of total disconnection.

Life melted into a series of pain waves. Thankfully, they began to dissipate and occasionally I had brief interludes of minor clarity of mind. During these free moments I realized you had been broken in several places. One of the breaks was an open fracture which exposed bone and almost forced the surgeons to cut you off. Instead, they had done a radical procedure, installing a titanium tibia in you. My body tried to reject the foreign material, but they did what was necessary to help you keep it. It was my only chance to walk on two feet.

I began having a verbal and internal dialogue with you. I let you know I loved and appreciated you and encouraged you to heal. In order to deal with the pain, I pictured you with normal blood flow and once again being a strong healthy bone. I continually envisioned myself upright and walking.

Soon my relationship with crutches began, one very similar to ours, the 'double-edged sword type.' I needed them yet I despised them. The Physio department discharged me as soon as I mastered the movement of going up and down five stairs.

The first day home as I hopped past my fridge, the magnets flew off sticking to your cast. I removed them realizing I needed to keep you away from magnetic forces. The sight of the airborne magnets terrified my toddler. But, when my seven year old witnessed the magnets take flight, he rolled on the floor in hysterics.

During the next nine months, along with riding the waves of pain, I developed the ability to proficiently (yet with a gentle and swift technique) capture my toddler with the crutches and later with a cane. My oldest child suffered greatly, sharing and shouldering the burden of pain and the lack of mobility you created. You were a major contributor to my son growing old before his time.

Still you had not mended, so they did another cutting edge surgery, a bone graph. It was going to take the pain away, and free me to dance again. During that hospital stay, a nurse shared with me that 'Messing around with one's bones is the most painful thing a human being can endure.' She instructed me in the art of pain management. I hopped out weeks later, drug free and once again, you were casted.

While cleaning up from our first post-bone graph dinner, you brought me to my knees with a forceful breath-taking stabbing pain. Not wanting to upset the kids, I acted like I was playing, dancing on my crutches. The next morning as I drove to school, you stole my breath away again - it was as though you had bitten me. By lunch hour the biting pain had happened multiple times. In between each chomp you were sharpening your teeth, warming up your jaw, readying to sever yourself from me. No pain management technique could battle the biting. I found myself heading for the fracture clinic, soon to be dubbed the *torture chamber*. Hours later, I was relieved to hop in and present my dilemma to the surgeon. Minutes later, I was in my car recalling how the surgeon had patted me on the head saying, 'Go on home this is not a pain-free process.'

I spent that evening and early morning in a state of feverish agony. It was as though you had fallen prey to billions of tiny carnivorous beasts. I was out of my mind! It was clear to me you had the potential to kill me or send me into a state of permanent lunacy. When the children woke, I instructed them to get in the car, buckle up, and wait for me. They were horrified, as my voice was unrecognizable. I was perspiring heavily, and you were letting loose a stomach-churning odour.

I plunged you into the tub full of water, and begged the children to get into the car because I had to go to the doctor. The ride was daunting. A thick fear-induced silence filled the vehicle. The unnatural unidentified odor you emitted oscillated throughout the car every few moments.

Upon arrival I told the nurse I had fallen in the tub. She brought the children and me directly inside the *torture chamber*. The surgeon let out a heavy sarcastic sounding sigh as he told me his assistant would be with me promptly and he would instruct him to remove the soaked cast.

I laid still and full of trepidation on the table in the centre of the room. My pyjama-clad children clutched the sides of the table and stared wide-eyed at me. The surgeon's assistant entered the room shortly after and began tearing the remnants of your cast away, plopping it on the floor. After a few pulls the stench overwhelmed our senses. The children began gagging and I hollered at them to wait outside.

The surgeon's assistant kept his thick brown hair and beard at medium length and dressed in traditional medical green scrubs. After he tore away a few more handfuls of the wet cast, I witnessed his face turning green. It coloured similar to the way people blush, fast and furious. But his flush started out a lime green hue, turned a tone darker than his scrubs, and finished a rich spinach shade. All this colouring was clearly visible through his beard. He left the room mumbling he would return quickly. The doctor came in moments later, asserting we had a little problem, and he would clean it up for me.

I caught sight of the little problem he was referring to. You had a gangrenous area, thick as a hockey puck and close to the same diameter; it concealed my shin. Simultaneously I felt profound pins and needles gallop all over me. I was out of my body floating as my head softly hit the table. I roused, to see the surgeon brandishing a long-handled pair of tongs that held an over sized cotton puff. He poured what smelled like bleach on the puff. As I heard the overflow splattering on the floor he told me we would begin.

The procedure of scrapping the gangrene away began. The pain you previously inflicted on me was mild compared to this process. I loathed you then and have continued my love/hate relationship with you ever since.

As I close, the phrase 'no pain no gain' comes to mind.

Ever enjoying learning to love you,

Joie

#20. Study Questions

Food for Thought

1. What part of herself is Joie addressing in this Letter? Elaborate on a similar experience you have had or of which you have known.

2. Joie mentions a nurse who taught her 'the art of pain management.' Discuss how and why it was important to Joie that the nurse did this.

3. Write two different sequel letters to 'Double-Edged Sword Type.'

Matters of the Heart

1. How were Joie's children affected by her injury?

2. Share the circumstances surrounding an incident when you felt a 'thick fear induced silence.'

#21. Shadow of Exhaustion

This is a love letter, not a romantic one, none-the-less a love letter.

Your physical beauty was stunning. Your skin had an opulent yet light caramel hue, a pleasing sight next to your lush brunette hair and your long slender ballerina-like form. Your deep brown almond-shaped eyes accentuated your high cheekbones - they brought to mind a beacon, both a guiding and warning light. Your air of humble affirming grace overwhelmed me - I had to bite my lip hard to stop it from quivering every time I looked at you. It was not your actions themselves that moved me to want to weep, but rather the shadow of exhaustion that tagged along beside you.

The way you kept your home was lovely as well - not a *fancy pants* sort of spot, rather an immaculate, modest place where even the ashtrays glittered. I was plagued with guilt during those times when you insisted I sit while you prepared a sandwich for me. I was not the good girl you thought me to be. In the kitchen you could make something special out of nothing. I often wondered how it was possible for a simple sandwich to taste so delicious.

Your fatigue shrouded my security with shame, for I knew you moved to my town from the Big Smoke after the crime that put our Capital City on the Gruesome City list. It became the City where four perverted men lured a young naive Shoe Shine boy into a den of sexual torment. Then after hours of battering the petite twelve year old, they held him over a sink, drowning him.

In my way of thinking at the time, the horrendous murder of this Shoe Shine boy turned my life from pathetic to perfect. A family lost their son and gained horrifying haunting memories, while my new love (who used to be a Shoe Shine boy) made my every moment safe. Fear, hatred and prejudice swarmed the City like locusts, altering the physical landscape and permanently scarring the hearts of the population. The friendly reputation was lost; protesters marched demanding the Prime Minister bring back the death penalty. I was doubly disgusted with myself since I gained love as a result of the vile actions of four perverted men.

I longed to cuddle with you. I wanted you to teach me how to cook and keep a beautiful house. Yet I did my best to stay clear of you, for I could not block the images of the dead boy when I saw you. Your son provided me with purpose and protection – I thought I did not deserve my romantic Knight in Shining Armour. I supposed deep down I was super scummy to revel in the love.

This summer, (almost 40 years later) my husband and I stood together in sober silence on the corner where he had laboured as a Shoe Shine boy. My husband cracked the quiet, commenting on how proud of his grey hair he is. He reminisced how at times he had made $80 a day down there - that was more than an average adult cleared in those days.

He wondered how the nice man who ran the major newspaper stand had made out after everything was shut down. He recanted the material tools he needed to make a good buck - the stool, the tins of black, brown, and neutral shoe polish, the polishing rags and of course the money-stashing tube socks. It went without saying his charisma, bravado, and good looks, coupled with his polished *gift of gab* were his social tools – his money makers. Yet, it was his sixth sense, the power we called our 'Spidee Sense' that most likely got him home to you at night unscathed.

Thank you for bringing my future husband to me. Our life together is even better than I ever imagined in my tween-aged daydreams. You were an exquisite woman with an enduring spirit, rich in sisterly, motherly and grandmotherly love. I will be sure to share pea soup with your great grandchildren, letting them know it was one of your favourites, filling their bellies, memories and hearts with your courage and vigour.

Love Joie

#21. Study Questions

Matters of the Heart

1. Discuss paragraphs five and eight of this Letter and consider:
   (a)　Why Joie refused to spend time with the woman?
   (b)　How is the 'Shadow of Exhaustion' brought to light?
   (c)　How did Joie feel about her gift of romantic love?
   (d)　In what way does Joie honour the memory of the woman?

#22. Worldly Wizard

This is a love letter, not a romantic one, none-the-less a love letter.

You are an extremely kind-hearted and fun-loving person who has always been a steady staple in my life - thank you for treating me so well.

In order to avoid attending high school in the City you stayed with us. The tale of you and the tenacious toddler began then. We had assigned seats and your breakfast included me assaulting your ears, jabbering insults while the sunlight blinded you. I am sure your teenage brain did not appreciate your senses being flooded like that upon awakening.

My early recollections of you were you being left-handed, and you had two super-neat habits I wanted to emulate. One was a suave way of flipping your hair to the side, and the other was a type of clicking sound you periodically released. I was also certain you had magical powers; I likened you to a friendly wizard, one who inspired laughter and awe.

Wherever we were eating you always had a special seat at the end of the table, as someone would declare, 'Stick that lefteee at the end!' I felt bad for you and gathered if being a lefty was something you could have changed, you would have.

I practised diligently to mimic your super-neat habits, only ever being able to achieve an exaggerated impression of your hair flipping move. I would lean my entire body to the right, aim my chin for my right shoulder, run my left hand through the bulk of my hair, parting it at the side tugging it upward and finally flicking my wrist to fling it back. The whole time thinking I was being debonair like you. Every night, for many nights, I repeatedly attempted to copy the quiet comforting clack-like sound you made. I inspected you thoroughly multiple times in hopes of spotting your tongue to see how you twisted it. I tried to no avail, begging my brain to grant me the power to make that sound. In the end, I accepted it was a wizardly way and so it would always be out of my realm of abilities.

Time after time the stories, card tricks and jokes you pulled off left me in a state of rapturous amazement. I did not know anyone else capable of such feats. That is how I knew you had wonder-working powers. Someone told me it really was no big deal, you were just doing tricks. I knew that was not true. It was a trick when I would be fooled into turning my eyes away from my supper only to look back and see lots of my food missing. You were born kind. You would not dupe me.

As I matured, my perception of you changed from wizardly to worldly, from mysterious to mild-mannered. Yet I have always wanted to take on some of your characteristics: your excellent parenting style, your solid work ethic, your giving ways in relationships, your generous nature, and of course how you *work* a room.

I will always consider you my very own wise wizard.

Love Joie

#22. Study Questions

Matters of the Heart

1. As a young child what adult did you find to have wonder-working powers? And what were those powers?

2. Who is your very own Wise Wizard? Why?

#23. Tween Over

This is a love letter. Life pushed us apart but our hearts did not stray.

We were a strong pseudo-family, you and I the couple, he the brother. We were closer than any family I have known. We referred to ourselves as tight, and declared our love for each other openly. He was satisfied that he had set us up, even though he constantly complained I was 'Just a stupid girl.' Aside from our private kissing sessions we functioned as a trio, every plan we enacted was for the betterment of us all, and we all suffered when our schemes backfired.

I met terror the first night things went down wrong, a type of terror I would come to know intimately – terror born of self-made disasters. I was *keeping six* as planned by pretending to talk on the payphone that had a clear view of the *job*. I expected the phone to ring within three or four minutes and hear your voice letting me know everything was a go. The silence of the phone was deafening. As more time passed, my adrenalin was reaching dangerous heights, making it difficult to keep cool.

I reminded myself of the reasons why my job was to *keep six*: my Spidee Sense was superb, my sense of smell was unusually potent (making it virtually impossible for anyone to sneak up on me), I could compel my breath to silence, I was a pro in the heat of the moment (that was my thing) and I could run like the wind. Most importantly I was *solid* - you and our brother were counting on me.

Just as I mentally composed myself, my Spidee *Sense* informed me to put down the phone and go lay in my cover spot. I sprawled belly down like a soldier in the tall grass surveying the area. When I heard the sirens closing in my adrenalin crash-landed, bouncing up into fear's grip. I did not think it was possible for them to get us, but I watched two of them manhandle you to the ground, cuff you and throw you in the back of the police car. Our *partner* had escaped but they had you!

Fear released its grip and my hatred of authority mushroomed as I watched the cruiser drive away. I endured my first serious session of self-pity based regret lying in the tall grassy cover spot. The pain was excruciating, as though a hive of super powered bees were taking turns at my flesh, their stingers hotter than a bonfire. I stayed still, holding tight my tears – it was not a time for crying.

Questions pounded their way through the pain every few seconds. How can we have our four children now? How will I be able to look at your Mom again? Will they beat him? Will he be out soon? How will I survive without his kisses? Will they make him eat garbage? Why had my plan failed? Is he going to drop me and get a new *Old Lady*? Why did they take him? Who will hide my naked body while I change my clothes? What did I do wrong? How can I go on without being able to smell you? I smashed my forehead several times against the ground where I had concealed myself. I commanded my brain to stop racing and my body to get moving to find you. I bolted over to the building where I assumed they had taken you.

I was determined to get a look at you. I stood motionless outside the centre all night. Around noon the next day I got a glimpse of you. We were slick non-verbal communicators, so even though you did not directly face me, I knew the glance we had of each other said all there was to say.

After seeing you I could not be still anymore, I had to run. I did not run to our *partner* as planned. Instead, I ran to oblivion, bee-lining away from everyone and everything. I did not care how I got there, only that I needed relief. I did my best to stay in no-man's-land until you returned.

I think you came back quickly that first time, but while you were gone the unthinkable had happened. I vowed never to tell you. We were together again and that was all that mattered. Our *partner* and his Mother knew exactly what happened in your absence. They both agreed we should not tell you, that it would ruin our love. It was my first and only secret from you.

When you got back, you told us they knew we were a troublemaking trio and that you had denied associating with us. They also had several things they wanted to pin on the three of us but we had outsmarted them. We were all now officially Juvenile Delinquents...

Love Always

Your Joie

#23. Study Questions

Food for Thought

1. Define and compare the terms Juvenile Delinquent, Young Offender and Youth at Risk.

2. Why did the term 'Juvenile Delinquent' become unacceptable?

3. When did the term 'Young Offender' become common?

4. What did changing these terms accomplish?

Matters of the Heart

1. Joie shared she endured a 'serious session of self-pity based regret' and compared the pain to being 'stung by a hive of super powered bees.' Describe a personal regret you have and what it feels like to you.

#24. Yearning & Waiting

This is a love letter. I yearned for you from the day we met - at last, I wait no more.

As youngsters we could not touch each other enough. I was elated to be in your arms. The scent of you awakened my sensual desires. I needed to be close to you, to kiss, cuddle and caress you. Being with you connected me to my place in our world; I was pleased to be a female, and looked forward to having a family. Every time we touched then, as now, it is both familiar and fresh. Each embrace is more exhilarating than before. We are always stunned by this, left bubbly-brained and pondering how is it possible? Each time our answer is the same - our skin is meant to mesh.

When circumstances separated us, I knew I would not feel solidly linked up in life without you. Unless time built a bridge or ledge where we could reach each other, I would have to pretend, act as if I was a genuine female.

Time inevitably moved on for more than a decade. Although I did enjoy life, I continually thought of you, pictured your face, and longed for you. The first few years that we were reunited were dreamlike. We were blinded by our love, and everyone near us felt its warmth. We have been together now almost longer than we were apart - the honeymoon is long over, yet we celebrate our love every day.

I am ecstatic to be a woman. Each day I wake full of dignified pride, my life is productive and purposeful. We are wealthy in the most valuable commodity - love.

The universe blessed us with a miraculous moment -
an archway unfolded for us to walk through and meet
again.

Yearning & Waiting

Getting together gave our souls
the ultimate tuning
It made our minds turn our hearts
all-consuming
We talk and it flows back and forth
really grooving
Your touch is electric always leaving my
body zooming

Smelling you
mesmerizes my soul
you leave my body
rocking, rocking,
body and heart
all parts popping
Oh, oh how can it be?
love and want to the umpteenth degree...

I get to be with the man of my dreams
You are the one who sews my exposed seams
You create seamless stitches throughout me
Showing me that I can love and be free

Tasting you
hypnotizes my soul
you leave my body
rocking, rocking,
body and heart
all parts popping

Feeling you
soothes my soul
you leave my body
rocking, rocking,
body and heart
all parts popping
Oh, oh how can it be?
love and want to the umpteenth degree...

Love Always

Your Joie

#24. Study Questions

Food for Thought

1. Critique the poem within this Letter literally and thematically taking into consideration:
   - (a) the title
   - (b) the tone
   - (c) the structure
   - (d) the sound and rhythm of the imagery.

#25. 3 Heartbeats

This is a love letter, not a romantic one, none-the-less a love letter.

You are the smallest person I have ever held, weighing in at five pounds and two ounces. I am awe struck now when I see you, a full-grown beautiful woman. They labelled you premature - I think you arrived exactly when you wanted to, with a deliberate and determined intention. I was nervous at the thought of holding you, yet our first embrace was so easy. An innate comfort level existed, one I have only shared with a handful of other people. Even today, no matter how much time passes that I do not see you, I am at ease in your presence, able just to be.

I had been with child for approximately six months then - it seemed somehow supernatural to hold you atop my baby bump. Caught in a reverie, I envisioned the three heartbeats pounding out a hypnotic rhythm. My heartbeat had the strong slow steady beat, yours was gentler and faster and the tiniest heart pounded with a subtle flurry. I introduced you to my unborn, sang to you both and vowed to protect the two of you with all the love and brawn I could muster. I wanted you to grow up knowing the daily sense of strong affection I had for you. I wanted you to always trust me. I loved being there those first few weeks you were home, having the opportunity to bond with you and for you and my baby to know each other in that unique way.

Eventually I returned to my home almost one hundred kilometres away, but I visited often and was thrilled with your development. It was not long before your premature birth was a non-issue. Everyone was well pleased that I had a son, a lone boy to mix with all the girls. Within the next few years more girls were born, including my baby girl. Holiday gatherings passed quickly then and we would talk on the phone and send mail to each other. You were a stubborn and studious girl - these traits have served you well as you matured in life.

Our Matriarch died, and you moved almost four thousand kilometres away a few days after the funeral. I was scared we would lose our connection, and suffered from not being able to see you. We continued our correspondence through the mail and on the telephone. You were so young that your accent changed quickly. The sound was sweet yet I was melancholy when I started hearing the linguistic transformation.

Some years later when the children and I came to visit, I tried to entice you to take a day off school to join us on an outing. You refused, not wanting to blotch your perfect attendance record. We went ahead without you, which infuriated you. You gave us your smart-alecky silent treatment for several days after, forgiving us in time for a tearful good-bye.

Typically, during your tween-age time you became closer with your peers and pulled away from those who lived afar. The letters slowed down, phone conversations got shorter and shorter. This did not disturb me, but I was concerned that my tight-knit relationship with your mother might make you uneasy with me. I wanted you to feel comfortable to confide in me, so I was delighted to receive my invitation to your high school graduation. I borrowed the money to get there and have pictures and mementos from the ceremony. You have always been a hard working independent young woman, who did not stray into a party way of life as many teens do. You were diligent with your college studies.

Sadly, I could not be there when your son was born. Thankfully, with the aid of today's technology, I was able to see pictures of your family within minutes of his arrival. You were so sweet to me about two years later when I did get to fly out, taking me shopping, going out of your way to bring your family to meet me. I held the heart-changing sound of your son's voice tight in my memory after that.

I was ecstatic at the prospect of you moving back. Your second child would be born here, and the new generation could grow up together. I am sorry I was sick when you first arrived - being unable to drive to help you broke my heart. As I held your baby girl very shortly after her birth, a sense of ease and comfort swept over me, reminiscent of how I felt the day I first held you.

My love for you and your family is infinite. In closing I must tell you, I love the big case of the warm fuzzies I feel when I hear you call your children by their pet names, Momma and Poppie.

Love Joie

#25. Study Questions

Matters of the Heart

1. Joie stated, 'Even today, no matter how much time passes that I do not see you, I am at ease in your presence, able just to be.' Who do you feel this way about in your life? What is it about this relationship that makes these feelings possible?

2. What gives you a 'big case of the warm fuzzies?' Describe and discuss these feelings.

#26. The Business with the Bunny

This is a love letter, not a romantic one, none-the-less a love letter.

I do not recall seeing you until the day you invited me into your life. Later you told me you had been watching me, witnessing the train wreck in action. That day you gave me a home - somewhere I could search out clean boxcars, build fresh track and get a new train running, my own train.

As you approached me (even though you were an old geezer) I found you to be a very handsome man. Your swagger, your long dark ponytail and matching beard comforted me. I appreciated your blunt manner of speech.

Your gaze disturbed me though - I had to look away after a split second. Your bright clear blue eyes bore through me, stirring the darkness within me. With one look, you seemed to recognize the filthy loneliness that was plaguing me. I thought you knew the steamroller of horror that I really was. Yet even so, you invited me to your home - I was dumbfounded and suspicious. I had been holding on to my new life with a death grip, therefore I figured I had nothing to lose by going with you.

I was seventeen then and old before my time in many ways. But during the short ride to your home I had a realization - I was just like an unhappy baby. The only needs I could identify were hunger and fear. What I could not fathom then was the incredible opportunity you were giving me. The ideal environment for me to live in, a safe place where I could go through my infancy, be free to cut my teeth.

You fed me a spiritual way of life, piecemeal, in small enough portions that I could digest. This new life was one of good manners, decent morals, a strong work ethic, healthy respect, family loyalty, pure laughter and a novel type of love.

It took me some time to learn how to shake hands properly, sit with others, eat gracefully and to engage in polite conversation. I wanted you to be proud of me so I began to practice these skills with a sense of urgency.

Through sharing your experience, you were able to instill in my mind a clear picture of socially acceptable norms. I learned right from wrong. At your table, over coffee, I decided not to sit on the fence where I was teetering but to jump down on the right side for a change. Thank you for bracing my fall. I have been able to live, to be free and to serve life because you were there.

I was amazed at how you made time for everyone even while working shift work and was stunned to discover you worked at a beer factory! I did my best to keep our agreement. I *got a lunch pail*, started back to school and although I did not want to work around beer, one of my goals was to become a valuable employee.

You wanted to know me. You spent one-on-one-time listening to me, and made certain when others were around I was included in the conversation. You treated me as an equal we were even-steven in your books that type of respect was foreign to me. I could not imagine I had anything valuable to say, so those times you asked me to talk, my stomach quivered and my flesh rolled. I was damned uncomfortable. You assured me you understood, and that if I stuck to it, one day my skin would settle, eventually it would fit.

I dreamt of marrying a man like you, as your wife was your one and only, your leading lady. It was clear you adored her - I was an eyewitness to your love, your dedication, the dancing, flowers and private talks into the wee hours. You worked hard for your family, which manifested in the hunting, fishing, camping and travel you enjoyed together. You were rugged yet affectionate with all of them, a perfect paradox for me to be privy to.

I was devoid of laughter and felt seriously scorned every time it erupted. As a result, I spent a great deal of my time alone sulking and sweating when all of you were busting a gut. I did not know why you believed I could make some headway in life but I knew you thought there was hope for me. You told me of some of your struggles. I felt your zest for life and I longed to laugh as well.

I think it may have been around the time of my 'business with the bunny' that I knew for sure you meant me no harm and that there were no perverse chains with my name on them hidden at your house. I had asked your permission to have one of the bunnies in my room for a time (it must have been something I needed for a school project). You granted my request and a bunny in a cage appeared in my room.

When I attempted to pick the bunny up I became petrified. I could not cope with the sensation of its heartbeat against my hands. I was like a dog learning the boundaries of its invisible fence. If I touched the bunny I had to let go and flee fast. I was wound up and waited for you to advise me, in hopes you would remove the bunny. You listened to me whining angrily, spewing all kinds of profanity about the bunny. I grumbled it was freaking me out, giving me the willies. I could not handle the bunny because in fact it was electrocuting me every time I tried to touch it. I begged you to take it away. You said, 'No darlin, the bunny stays.' I was livid; I held your gaze and stood stiff as steel. You gently cupped my hands inside one of yours and explained, 'That floppy eared critter will help you to understand that you are alive.'

As you left me, I realized we had maintained eye contact and I did not get squeamish, and that when you called me 'darlin' I stood tall as the tallest of trees. After this 'business with the bunny', I stopped sliding my bed and dresser in front of the door every night. I even wanted to laugh a few times. I know I trusted you then, felt connected to you. As a duckling imprints at birth, my love for you had commenced. Thank you a million times over for taking me in. Surely I would have died or been locked away forever if I had not had that time with you.

Years passed and though I moved away, I remained thankful for you every day and practised with perseverance the skills you taught me. Later you entered my life, vicariously at first, being there for my one and only, my leading man. I could not think of anyone I would have sooner seen him involved with. Thanks to you, we had hope.

You and I were able to enjoy time together, talking, sharing meals and finally I could laugh! In fact, most times when I would leave your presence my face was sore from smiling so much. I found that in a certain way, the tables had turned. I did not long for you to be proud of me but rather I was well pleased to be with you.

It was sweet of you to give me your sweatshirt, the one that reads 'I'm not 40 just 18 with 22 years of experience.' You told me it had resurfaced and because you had never seen anyone so happy to turn forty, you thought I might like it. You were right of course. I love to wear your shirt.

A few years back you helped me put new wires and switches in my lamps. It was a fun afternoon, one of my many wonderful memories of our times together. The lamps mean a great deal to me now. Similar to the spiritual force you shared with me, they illuminate the room along with anyone and anything in it.

I love you,

Joie

#26. Study Questions

Food for Thought

1. Using the text and your own interpretation, write a paragraph describing the man in this Letter.

Matters of the Heart

1. Joie stated, 'and when you called me darlin I stood as tall as the tallest of trees.' What is the statement another person makes which makes you feel this way? And why?

2. Describe a scenario where you have been helped vicariously. How does the scenario reinforce the notion that the actions of another person can have a ripple effect?

#27. Belly Button

This is a love letter, not a romantic one, none-the-less a love letter.

You were there ensuring I was born safely that early June morning. Since I know you cut my umbilical cord, I think fondly of you every time I notice my belly button. I love the fact you were my official baby catcher. As a GP in those days, you took care of so much, even making house calls. Your intellect was above average and you had an affectionate disposition, a rare mix of character.

We lived in the same area for twenty years after my birth. Thank you for always being there to help me, and for treating me without prejudice. I was deeply remorseful for the hurt I must have caused you, and extremely happy I had time to redeem myself in your eyes - to make amends. It must have been distressing for you to see such a young girl in the state I was in, especially considering the type of bond we shared.

It is safe to assume you did not know what I had been up to until the day they called you to the school. They had never had a problem of that nature - after all it was a primary school in a small town. Of course, my memory of the incident is hazy, yet I know when you called out to me I opened the door. People had been desperately pounding on the door and resorted to uttering threats to try to get me to open it. I did hear some muffled sounds but was oblivious to their significance. I sat stretched back with my feet up, hell-bent on inhaling what I was smoking. Your voice rang through my mind clearly and as you asked, I wobbled towards the door and opened it. Before the ambulance drove away I recall you proclaiming you would see me at the hospital and we would make a plan.

At the hospital, a peculiar sense of irritation and emptiness ran up my nose, through my nasal cavity and down the middle of my chest. My throat was on fire, as though a white-hot ember was burning in it. A suction/pumping sound was annoyingly echoing in my mind. My body felt as thin as an inch thick sheet of metal, and as worn down as the asphalt on a major highway.

During that short hospital stay I learned firsthand of a new world, one I had only seen as a visitor. It was a place of needles and tubes – a space with one-way mirrors and observation rooms. There were weird doctors and wide-open camera-clad washrooms. In this strange space people shrieked when they were being unbound, shuffled rather than walked, and most seemed oblivious to their own existence.

As you promised, you came to see me. Your voice was brimming over with care and concern – the sound of it triggered one of my many colossal guilt attacks. You let me know you had the power to have me placed in a secured setting similar to where I was, except it was specifically for children and it was a few hundred miles away. I did not want to go far away so I promised you I would be good from here on out. You told me what you wanted me to avoid and some new things you wanted me to try and I agreed to your terms. Thank you for being so kind-hearted.

After that, I avoided you, as fourteenth century royalty fled the black plague. Even though I wholeheartedly wanted to keep the promises I made to you, I knew then that I could not, and I expected I would never be capable of doing so.

At the end of my eight year *run,* when I called for help, your spouse took the call. I doubted my ability to change but was willing to do anything the two of you suggested. Your partner prompted me to write a basic list of what I was to do and not do, and to look at it before making any decisions. I referred to the list faithfully before taking any action. Eventually I lost the paper I had written the list on, but day by day the list swells...

Love Joie

#27. Study Questions

Food for Thought

1. Write a scenario to describe what may have happened between Joie and the paramedics during her ambulance ride.

2. Write a dialogue between Joie and the hospital staff who treated her upon arrival.

Matters of the Heart

1. In paragraph seven Joie states she whole-heartedly wanted to keep the promises she made her GP and she knew she couldn't. Describe a time when you whole-heartedly wanted to keep a promise to someone and knew you couldn't or a time when you have heard someone else who made a promise they were unable to keep.

2. Why do you think the sound of the GP's voice triggered one of Joie's many colossal guilt attacks?'

#28. Dam

This is a love letter, not a romantic one, none-the-less a love letter.

My *partner* brought me to you, wanting to put me somewhere safe so he could go and even the score. I was numb, bloody and broken. Thank you for helping and for not exposing me. Your wisdom prevented him from violently retaliating, and it was adhesive to my wounds.

Although I was with you for quite some time, you spoke little and barely touched me. I know your experiences had equipped you with clean gloves that were the ideal texture to handle me. I likely may have sought out *marketeers* to surrender myself to if you had not nursed me that evening.

but it was a dirty glove

During my first meeting with you a few months prior I was witness to your superior physical resilience. The first time your son (my *partner*) brought me to your apartment some dastardly violent action went down. We hid in the hall closet waiting for a chance to help you. Clinging together, sweltering like popsicles in the sun, I feared the stream of sweat running onto the floor would break our cover.

I thought your head was going to come clear off that day! As soon as your attacker left we came to your aid. You told us to get away quickly in case it started again. Later your son told me you were very tough, that you had taken even worse beatings and stood right back up.

Even if I had not seen what happened that day I would have known just how durable you were by looking at you. Although you had a small build you moved in a commanding manner. Your walk conveyed a clear message; I may have been born into a man's world but I am going to walk my way straight through it.

I went for a ride in his van
He showed the prerogative of a man

Your words to me then were commands and assurances - I readily followed your instructions and thought I would be safe with you. You guided me to get in the mustard bath letting me know it would feel soothing and ensure my body stayed to its own. You promised you would sit on the other side of the door with your back to it. I heard you tell your boy to go and burn the clothes I had on, to find something loose fitting and warm for me to wear, and not to forget the belt and maxi pads.

Later, when you placed a shot of rye and a sandwich in front of me I could only supp and peck at them. I found it seriously strange that I did not gulp the rye and seek more. As you both slept, I sat idle except when I needed to replace a soiled maxi pad with a white one. I collected the stained ones in the dark plastic bag you had given me, gripping it between my feet as though it were the last cup of water on earth.

Days passed and the need to change the pads diminished. I began to come back to myself. Although altered, I was able to remember how to behave. We agreed the best course of action was business as usual. I was pleased with this plan and pumped to get back in the *action*.

Dam

I'm 14, I don't think I can be tricked
I am tough, people like me are not picked
Victims are those soft weak and pampered girls
Girls laughing, wearing skirts and doing swirls

I'm not hot, I'm not even feminine
I never thought this story would begin
I turned 14 with my virginity
That night he pushed his body into me

one of my friends helped me clean up the blood
we burned the clothes to dam the memory flood

I went for a ride with him in his van
He showed the prerogative of a man
The first part of my birthday present was
smoking, drinking, getting a bigger buzz

Then he smirked, showed me condoms and I knew
I was weak, as weak as the morning dew
He reminded me of how strong he was
And that I wanted this just like the buzz

one of my friends helped me clean up the blood
we burned the clothes to dam the memory flood

He willed and paralyzed me on my back
I went void not to give him any flack
When he turned around with that condom on
and made me look, my heart and soul went gone

I was a teeny tiny bug
hovering there up above
he said that this was some love
but it was a dirty glove

clean up the blood
dam the memory flood
clean up the blood
dam the memory flood

The girl is not a virgin any more
The man pushed his body, her choice he tore
She seemed to be dying, bleeding in pain
He said he was proud her cherry he gained

She wrenched as he put her pants back on her
He said she knew what happened was a blur

one of my friends helped me clean up the blood
we burned the clothes to dam the memory flood

clean up the blood
clean up the blood
dam the memory flood
dam the memory flood

one of my friends helped me clean up the blood
we burned the clothes to dam the memory flood

Of the numerous accounts I could write to you, this is the one I long to share the most. Thank you for the way you nursed me then, your gentle understanding and no-fault-attitude empowered me to forgive and accept myself.

With a grateful heart,

Joie

#28. Study Questions

Food for Thought

1. Critique the poem within this Letter literally and thematically considering:
(a) the title
(b) the choice and placement of tense
(c) the structure.

Matters of the Heart

1. How do you feel about the way the woman chose to act when Joie was brought to her?

2. In paragraph two Joie mentions the woman who helped her had 'clean gloves that were the ideal texture to handle me.' What does it mean to you if another has gloves the ideal texture to handle you?

#29. Donut Shop Duo

This is a love letter, not a romantic one, none-the-less a love letter.

I do not think I ever knew your names, yet I clearly remember you both. Thank you for reaching out to me. Even though I never did see the two of you together, I nicknamed you, my Donut Shop Duo.

I was spinning on a stool in the donut shop when my blackout ended. As I returned to consciousness my stomach began to reel. I slammed my feet on the ground and high-tailed it to the washroom where I proceeded to vomit with great bravado.

Sometime later as I plopped myself back onto the seat, I noticed you were sitting a few spaces over. You, the male part of my Donut Shop Duo, were a man with a small physique - not much taller than I was yet most likely double my weight. Your dark hair and irises complimented your round eyes.

You began to tell me the story of when you and your wife were homeless. You had a fire in your place and many people helped you after that horrific event. Furthermore, you wanted me to know since recovering from the fire, you have tried to help others, and I could rest my head at your place for a while to get on my feet. I figured you were trying to lure me somewhere, to use me for something. Yet your pupils seemed to say the opposite, as they were steady and reasonably sized. That meant to me you were not drugged or adrenaline pumped, and that you were not likely full of lustful anticipation.

I was shaky, sick and very tired, so I agreed to accompany you home. After you unlocked the apartment door and pointed me in the direction of the couch I never saw you again. Thank you for being gentle with me, and for giving me a place to take a break.

Later, my sixth sense woke me - I opened my eyes to see you, the female part of my Donut Shop Duo taking a very close look at me, by sitting on the edge of the coffee table and leaning into me. I was taller than you, and I probably even outweighed you. I was taken aback by how much you resembled the man I thought was your husband - you could have easily passed as brother and sister. Your hair and eyes were dark, but the creepy contrast was your small swiftly darting pupils.

You offered to get me food and drink - saying you were worried that I needed sustenance after sleeping for almost twenty-four hours. It was a challenge for me to pull my mouth open but once I did, I devoured everything on the tray you brought me.

It was perplexing that your movements and your manner of speech flowed in an average way, yet your pupils moved in that odd rhythm. I decided I had better get out of there while the getting was good. When I told you I had to leave, you implored me to wait a while, saying I could stay as long as I wanted. I gently explained people were expecting me so I had better hit the road.

You brought a six-pack out of the fridge, placed it on my lap, and suggested I stay at least until you could go shopping to get me a few things. You had determined your shoes were too big for me, and I should not be running about in bare feet. One of the beers was smoothly sliding down my gullet when you dropped a change of clothes, a toothbrush, a towel and your keys on the couch beside me. You left shouting for me to lock the door and reminding me we had the apartment to ourselves for the next couple of days.

I was powered-up as I slid the chain lock closed and clicked the deadbolt down. I made sure the lock was tight on the glass sliding doors and headed for the bathroom. The shower and change of clothes were invigorating. I was delighted to have used conditioner to aid in taming my tangles.

Thank you for giving me time alone in your home, for those hours I was lost in a domestic daydream. It was pleasant for me to pretend I had my own place. The apartment had a lived in feel to it, as it was modest and tidy. The balcony faced one of my favourite parks (the one with a beautiful and historical green house on site.) I gazed out the glass doors, people watching.

I imagined maybe one day I would carry a purse, and that it would contain make-up, and of course, there would be a wallet in it. The wallet would always have a crisp $50 bill in the billfold. Whenever I made a purchase, I would flip down the photo section and fan out the lovely photos of my family. I could see myself opening the inside zipper of the purse to pull out my set of keys - the set that would hold my house keys.

Your tapping on the door snapped me out of my fantasy - I peered through the peephole to make certain it was you. You were talking really fast, telling me to try on the sneakers you had bought me and asking me if I liked them, wondering if they fit.

You seemed genuinely delighted to have purchased a nylon bag, several pairs of underpants and socks, a couple of tee shirts, a hairbrush, sweat pants and a sweatshirt for me. As I crammed the two remaining bottles of the six-pack in with the contents of the bag, I assured you the gifts were perfect and it was great of you to have bought so much for me. I thanked you for having me over and apologized for being a burden.

As I ran down the staircase I almost tripped over a likeness of you. The hologram was a crystal-clear picture of you smiling wide as you pulled your wallet out of your purse to pay for what you had bought me. I hesitated, momentarily mesmerized by the image, before instinctively punching it with guilt-filled fists. The smack of my double-fisted punch cleared it out of my way so I could freely run on.

Thank you my Donut Shop Duo, for reminding me a man can act without malicious intent and a woman can enjoy shopping for a stranger. In your home I caught some much-needed rest, and a rare and fantastic chance to be free to dream.

Love Joie

P.S. My domestic dreams have been realized.

#29. Study Questions

Food for Thought

1. Why did Joie agree to go with the man to his apartment?

2. What age bracket was Joie in when the incidents in this Letter took place?

3. Rewrite the second last paragraph of this Letter sharing an instance of personal guilt. Be sure to include if you suppressed your guilt and for how long.

Matters of the Heart

1. How did you feel about the woman's decision to:
    - (a) give Joie a six pack of beer?
    - (b) to leave Joie alone in her apartment?
    - (c) to buy Joie shoes, clothes and toiletries?

#30. Impromptu Gab Session

This is a love letter, not a romantic one, none-the-less a love letter.

For a fourteen year span your voice was reassuring to me when I called, and you always greeted me with genuine concern. I did my best to let you know I thought you were the cat's ass and I appreciated your work.

When I could, I would pop in just to say hello and often times we would enjoy an impromptu gab session. During the years I wrote a few letters of praise to your superiors, telling them you ran your office professionally, effectively and everyone I talked to said they loved you.

The day I saw someone else in your place and heard you would not be back my tears fell on the spot. My throat did not tighten nor did my lip quiver; the tears just fell.

They ran down the bridge of my nose and off my face pelting my pants like miniature hail. They flowed in that manner on and off for several days. I was going to miss you and hoped I would be able to bump into you from time to time.

I was satisfied I had always shared with you how much I appreciated you and trusted that you would remember me fondly.

You had a challenging position, and you made it flow smoothly. You are one smart cookie. Thank you for the years of excellent service.

Love Joie

#30. Study Questions

Food for Thought

1. Compile a list of customer service jobs. Consider:
   - (a) how many customer service jobs have you or someone you love worked?
   - (b) rate the jobs in order of difficulty.

Matters of the Heart

1. Write a complimentary Letter to a customer service worker in your life and send a copy to their superior.

#31. Sparkler

This is a love letter, not a romantic one, none-the-less a love letter.

I miss you. Yet I am glad your suffering ended, as the hard times were brutal. I could love you easier now if I deemed your death solely to be a pleasant transition in my life. Your death was also an end to our physical time together; your absence is an open wound. I long for you to share in my triumphs, and there have been many since you passed. My accomplishments are accompanied by a lump of grief, my throat swells, stealing my breath, reminding me I cannot share the moment with you. I wish we could dance together and I did not have to rely on my memory to hear your strong baritone belting out the classic 1970's hits.

For the first twenty years of my life my connection to you was practically indestructible. During the first decade, my primary goal was to get you to give me the sparkly-eyed look. I knew my behavior could cause your shoulders to puff up, a smile to slide across your lips, and your voice to ring tenderly. Yet making your eyes shine as a super sparkler on a pitch-black night was my true aim. I would have traded a whole pack of super-duper sparklers for one of those looks – it did not fizz out fast and give off a bad odor.

The sparkles that soared out of your striking brown eyes lingered long, similar to the way the sweet scent of our flowering lilac trees flowed throughout the house.

Our bond led me to understand many things of men; they were dark haired, handsome and strong as nails.

They kept their wives' shoes polished, and worked long and hard to give the money they earned to their families. I knew sometimes they drank too much, and they always had chain saws in the trunk of their cars.

I learned the remedy for shaky hands was a mixture of beer, tomato juice and an antacid. And of course hard work cured any problem. It made sense to me that remorse was fleeting and loose lips sank ships.

It was clear cars were meant to move fast, and any tree could be made to fall in a particular spot. I recognized although a real man could shed tears, it was not something to speak of. I also took for granted every man had some episodes of memory loss.

I had a keen awareness stealing was no problem, as long as it happened at the right time and place, and the same theory applied to swearing.

I believed men created and maintained ice rinks in their back yards, and they always shopped for Christmas on the eve of it - using newspaper to wrap their gifts. I knew men considered planting and tending a garden paramount and as vital as having black coffee and cigarettes every day.

It was obvious men had road maps built into their brains. They knew exactly how fast to thunder down tickle hills, ensuring their passengers squealed as their tummies flip-flopped. I accepted men had to get rid of the chair they passed the slow season in (due to the indent their weight had created in it) and furthermore the annual *chuck the chair tradition* was fun!

Through my confusion, I acknowledged sometimes Spring Fever overpowered men, and it took them away from their homes for a time. I appreciated occasionally men got caught up in something and could not make it home at night. When they did return, they may be black, blue and bloody, and their cars may be squished or missing.

I knew men loved their families more than they loved themselves. Clearly everything and anything good that happened to them was a direct result of their family's love.

At a reasonable age, I learned each man is actually unique, yet accepting that was a long drawn out emotional revolt for me. You were my King; I revered, adored, and admired you. I was in awe of you, and I knew you would shelter me at any cost. My love and loyalty for you was as rock-hard as a mountain-sized diamond. We were an invincible alliance, easily identified, with bounds impossible to breach...

#31. Study Questions

Food for Thought

1. How do you define co-dependency?

2. List some of the many things of men Joie learned from the man in this Letter.

3. What is the legal age in your area to:
   - (a) drive
   - (b) vote
   - (c) enter the military
   - (d) purchase cigarettes
   - (e) purchase alcohol
   - (f) be incarcerated in an adult correctional facility?

Matters of the Heart

1. What were some of your primary goals during the first decade of your life?

2. Who has loved you more than they have loved themselves? Why?

3. What is a reasonable age for one to realize that parental authorities are not perfect?

4. Which Matters of the Heart have been long drawn out emotional revolts for you? And why?

#32. Personal Private Haven

This is a love letter, not a romantic one, none-the-less a love letter.

I did not even know what you looked like when I fell in love with you, and I fell fast and hard. I have not met you (although I did make eye contact with you once in the late 1980's) but the chance we will meet is slim to none. Our relationship is worth a great deal to me. It sustained me through many trying times and gave me a permanent respite.

Your love hit me in 1979 as I sat by the Bay and it holds true to this day. I was laying on a soft green grassy incline when my friend placed the small boombox we shared beside me. He threw a cassette tape at me suggesting I check it out - he thought I might like it.

I could not have imagined what was in store for me as I clicked the tape into place, closed the door and pressed play. Your voice rang out and it triggered an immediate and lasting transformation in me. I was invigorated and at the same time a strong measure of tranquility came over me. I had previously enjoyed music and could recite many tunes. Now I understood the right music was mind-blowing. I knew I had found everlasting love (as soon as I could memorize it) I could be with it anytime. I would have a personal private haven, even shackles or a jail cell could not keep the music from me.

Eager to memorize every note, I played the tape until the batteries were worn out, and then I sought new ones as if they were the last drop of water on earth. My friend could not convince me to put the music aside - it was several days before I could stop playing the tape. After I memorized your vocals, I took in the sounds of the bass, lead guitar and drums - then I was satisfied, the music was with me forever.

I earnestly sought out all the recordings you had made, vowing to listen to them through a set of headphones. I desperately searched for people with stereo systems and the right record collections, begging them to let me have some headphone time. My friend was sorry he had turned me on to the tape. He claimed I went over the top with it. His favorite artist was not you, and so we had many heated discussions, each of us slamming the other's Rock God.

We were able to wait in line over night and purchase tickets to attend his rocker's show. Each of his freckles glistened and gave a rock and roll head-nod when we had the tickets in our hands. I was stoked to be accompanying him. The day of the concert he made certain to stay sober, wanting to remember every detail.

That night, I watched him more than the show and was intrigued by the unfamiliar smile that opened his face. An exquisite orange coloured aura, sprinkled with red and white swirls illuminated a foot from his chest, up and out, several feet over his head. Through the glow, he appeared angelic, handsome and at peace; for the first time since I had known him he had an air of sweetness. Today I understand music activates the release of Dopamine and Oxytocin in people. That is why at the concert he let his guard down, and why he was unusually friendly for almost a week after the show. In those days I simply believed in the paranormal power of the Rock Gods.

I had to resign myself to the fact I would never get to hear you live, so over the next five or so years I soaked in all of your music, and held on to it at times as a drowning person would adhere to a raft.

You produced a solo album which I became familiar with through my headphones and my remote controlled CD player. When your tour was announced I had no problem convincing someone with a credit card to purchase my ticket for me. A courier service delivered the ticket to my door and I was particularly preoccupied with its safety during the month long wait for the show. I was giddy with excitement, being especially keyed up for the concert.

Your show was taking place in the same venue where my friend and I had gone to hear his Rock God. Unfortunately he would join me in spirit only, as he had died tragically a few years earlier.

At your performance, I re-lived a more intense and enlightened version of the time by the Bay when I became hooked on you.

Thank you for giving me a personal private haven.

Love Joie

#32. Study Questions

Food for Thought

1. Discuss the many modes and methods of recording and listening to music since the advent of the phonograph? How was music shared before it could be recorded and reproduced?

Matters of the Heart

1. What is the force in your life that is invigorating and at the same time brings you a strong measure of tranquility? And why?

#33. Cat & Mouse

This is a love letter, not a romantic one, none-the-less a love letter.

I abhorred you with all my energy for a great deal of my life, yet now I write you a heartfelt love letter. I have the utmost respect for you, and do all I can to demonstrate that. Mostly, I try to show anyone you are possessing there is a peaceful way to co-exist with you, that indeed life can be fulfilling.

You are the pickpocket that snatched my soul when I was a child, playing an 8-year long game of cat and mouse with me. You tormented my mind, body and soul; I was under your authority completely, every move I made prompted by a swat from your razor sharp claws.

You ruled this way until I was on the brink of expiring, and at 17, I decided to find a way to end the *action*. I stopped playing dead and took up arms, eager to eliminate you. It was tough, a battle evermore, yet I was determined to win. I used any tool known to humanity to combat you - I held you at bay with one hand and manoeuvred through life with the other. Even though we were still skirmishing, (and it was exhausting) I was pleased, as I had stood up, and was deciding daily in which direction to move.

Almost a decade later, I let you overtake me again. For seven months, I stayed on the ground while you toyed with me, as a lion would with a wild boar. I did not know I was dying until I woke in the hospital and inquired as to how I came to be there. I learned you had conquered me, paralyzing my body, and a medical team had to jump-start my heart, to bring me back to life. I knew I was as thin and translucent as a single layer of plastic wrap. I could not fight you anymore, rather, I had to learn to live with you, to love you.

At first, it was a white-knuckle existence, which was painstaking considering I was as weak as the puniest runt of any litter, and my mind was constantly telling me to let you have your way with me. It seemed as if a cement blanket of shame encased me and I did not have the equipment or the expertise to shatter it. I leaned on those who came before me, and humbly began to look at you as a positive part of me, rather than a force to be reckoned with. Since then my capacity to love you has flourished. I am sincerely thankful we are in this life together.

Ever enjoying learning to love you,

Joie

#33. Study Questions

Food for Thought

1. Which other Letters share insights to understand the essence of this Letter? And what are those pieces of information?

2. What is the significance of the closing line 'Ever enjoying learning to love you?'

Matters of the Heart

1. When you were young or vulnerable did a pickpocket snatch part of your soul? Describe the journey of recapturing or claiming it.

#34. a-devil-of-a-time

This is a love letter, not a romantic one, none-the-less a love letter.

At first you wanted me to sell you on the idea of helping me, as you felt there was not enough clinical evidence to support taking any action. You were willing to perform another biopsy. I was not keen on lying still, letting you push a needle (one equipped with sets of flesh pulling pinchers) in between my collarbones. I insisted on an ultrasound instead. As I left the room, I sensed you did not expect to see me anytime soon.

The ultra sound took place two days later, and the following day you invited me back to talk with you. Your eyes were gentle, and your voice soft as you put it plainly, 'You must be having a-devil-of-a-time.' I was put on your cancellation list to ensure you could operate as soon as possible.

I was not getting enough oxygen, and was at risk of choking to death, but you had great confidence you could repair the problem. I was very frightened when you told me there was a slim chance I could have trouble singing and talking afterwards as you would have to set aside my vocal chords during the surgery. You explained you were very good at your job and had no reason to think anything would go wrong. I knew I would be a fool not to agree to have the operation. I looked forward to not choking frequently, being short of breath constantly, experiencing hours on end of lethargy and finding it increasingly difficult to move my neck.

The multiple surgeries I had had before all involved long painstaking recovery periods. This time I felt relieved as soon as I awoke. After the anesthetic washed out of my body, I felt better than I had in many years. My family and I greatly appreciate what you did for me. Thank you for dedicating many years of your life to intense training, for listening to me, and of course for saving my life.

Love Joie

#34. Study Questions

Food for Thought

1. Define clinical evidence.

2. How many years and approximately how much money does it cost someone to educate themselves as a GP? And as a specialist?

Matters of the Heart

1. The doctor told Joie there would be a slim chance she could have trouble singing and talking after the surgery. Discuss the notion of losing your ability to speak.

#35. Tea in the Shower

This is a love letter, not a romantic one, none-the-less a love letter.

The last time I laid eyes on you was around thirty years ago, but when I think of you a sinister stirring scurries up and down my spine - it is a gut churning and wrenching sensation. My heartstrings twist pretzel-like making it hard to breathe, and my mind is wrought with the same haunting image of you. You stand stately and faceless, wearing white tennis style shoes, sporting dark denim jeans, a blue tee-shirt with your cut-to-fit-by-you jean vest. Your long, one-length soaked hair almost reaches your lower back. A red neon sign flashes brazenly and endlessly a-top your head spelling out - why me?

The last time I remember being with you I screamed up into your window demanding you bring me down the stash you were holding for me. I was irrationally irritated with you for making me wait a few minutes while you showered. About ten minutes later, you appeared with your hair dripping and your favourite tea mug in hand. You gave me the details of how you had been enjoying your tea in the shower. You loved a hot cup of tea any time, but it was especially cool to have a hot shower and a hot tea simultaneously.

I was fuming, hearing you talk of your tea. I wanted you to pass me the stash so we could get down to business. As you drained your mug and hid it in the bush, I ridiculed you with the sharpest slang my teenaged tongue could spit out. You remained your usual cheery self as I slammed you, yet I bet it was not the first time I hurt you with my derogatory dialect. The truth was I knew you were a better person than me. You were fun-loving, not a ruffian, you were sweet to others and had a healthy conscience that kept you from crossing the clear lines you had drawn. You were what would now be called a geek, reaching *high score* on all popular arcade games, and showing excellent sportsmanship at the pool tables.

I crossed one of my own lines that day by being so mean to you. You were naive and soft. I knew I should have kept my distance from you, not bullied you any further. When I went straight, I remember thinking you would be proud, and after a reasonable time I would have to take the opportunity to apologize to you for my cruelty.

I found sticking to my guns as a straight-ass tough in our County so I moved away, started fresh. It was a wise choice, for my old life was no longer a shadow glaring at me through the eyes of others. I attained some post secondary education and had a family of my own, before deciding to move back.

I was thirty four when I bumped into someone who I thought would know of you. I cheerfully asked about your whereabouts and the response I heard struck my head like a side kick from a professional kick-boxer. My knees buckled. The person telling me about you held me steady for a time until I gained my footing.

Apparently, when we were 16, you had disappeared without a trace. There had been no worldwide manhunt for you, no flyers of your face posted, and you were not pictured on milk cartons throughout the world. You were considered just another teenaged runner.

I want you to know I have been a hard-core tea drinker since I went straight. When I was told of your disappearance I started enjoying tea when I soak in the tub, affectionately observing the small stream of steam that floats a-top my favorite mug as I drink its contents.

Salutations,

Love Joie

#35. Study Questions

Food for Thought

1. Research statistics on the number of missing marginalized youth in your area over the last three decades.

2. Discuss what factors contribute to a youth being considered 'At Risk.'

3. Compile a list of attributes describing the subject of this Letter including physicality and personality traits.

Matters of the Heart

1. Share an issue that 'twists your heartstrings pretzel-like making it hard for you to breathe.' What do you do to find peace of mind regarding this issue?

#36. Tiny Soldier

This is a love letter, not a romantic one, none-the-less a love letter.

I met you the day I was returning to the hospital after visiting the group home I was to reside in upon my discharge. It was the first train ride I paid for and I was bitterly disappointed. I was lonely and displaced, wishing I could be back at the hospital. I did not like the group home or anyone I met there during my two-night stay. I planned to convince the hospital staff to keep me there instead.

To end my trip I had to wait for an hour at one of my old stomping grounds. I felt odd, imagining myself a lone flower of bumpy broccoli misplaced into a beef and potato stew.

I decided it would be wisest for me to sit upstairs in the familiar terminal; I did not want an old acquaintance to recognize me and put me to the test. I doubted I had the gumption to profess my new way of life or to just say 'no.'

I plunked myself down on a bench upstairs feeling proud of my attire. I wore a hip headband, a retro quarter-length concert shirt, army style pants and tiny workmen-like boots. I was very fond of my black boots. For years I had been barefoot, now I was looking forward to having a long relationship with my boots. Although I thought the black nylon bag I borrowed for the trip was lame I knew it was better than carting my belongings in black garbage bags like I used to.

Sometime after I sat down a middle-aged man joined me a few spots away on the bench. He was unassuming, sober and did not even smoke cigarettes. He struck up a conversation. I found him easy to talk to. Considering we were the only people upstairs, I did not worry someone would hear our conversation. It felt liberating to share with him how I changed my life, and that as hard as the last few months had been I could see improvements in myself already.

I told him details of my condition, how I had been extremely close to death, but I looked completely restored now. The bright yellow glow of my eyes had turned white again, and my skin had shed its yellow hue. I let him know how pleased I was the swelling and pain in my side seemed to be subsiding. Also, one of my favourite nurses had really encouraged me to stay straight. She believed if I continued to abstain my pancreas might recover.

He thought me helping other young people was a great idea. He knew kids would come to me for advice and had no problem picturing me as a leader. He believed in no time at all I would be a real lady, dressed in skirts, moving in genuine leather lady-like boots. I was remarkably comforted and encouraged by this stranger, and thought he was really cool especially considering he was giving his own time freely to sit with me.

When he invited me to join him downstairs for lunch I declined, letting him know I had spent all my money on smokes and I was scared one of my connections would recognize me if I did not stay upstairs.

He showed me five 20 dollar bills in his wallet making it clear he could afford to buy me lunch, and assured me he would protect me from anyone who tried to bother me. I told him I would not feel right letting him buy me food. After a bit of debate we agreed to go sit in the restaurant together, that it would be okay for him to buy me a milkshake.

We sat at a booth - he faced the window to watch out for me. I tucked myself and my duffel bag in, trying to be inconspicuous. I was distressed downstairs, longing for the security of the hospital. Thankfully there was only a half hour left before my departure.

The milkshake was delicious. To stop myself from gulping it down, I began counting the flecks of strawberry floating in it, and when I looked up another man was sitting across from me. While I was engrossed in counting the pink particles, my new acquaintance had stood and let his friend slide into the booth. He said he was a good friend who had just happened by and wanted to join us.

The new man at the table was extremely different from the first - they did not seem likely friends. It was hard to estimate his age, his clothes were top of the line and he was rock-star style gorgeous. They both referred to me by name and not knowing their names I thought of them as One and Slick.

Having lost interest in the milkshake, I turned to check the clock and saw I had twenty minutes before I could get on the bus to head back to my safety zone.

One and Slick talked at length about me as if I was not across the table. They spoke of my strength and beauty and of how I was going to help loads of kids. Occasionally the newcomer would flash a potent smile and wink my way. I was embarrassed because his gaze was affecting me - I thought I might have been blushing. He nudged my knee and whispered he was going to pass me something under the table. I grabbed the piece of paper without looking at it and shoved it in one of the side pockets of my pants. I thought it was likely his phone number, yet I found it odd that he would make such a fuss just to pass me a number.

Perspiration began descending down my sides like a small landslide. When I cranked my neck to take note of the time the tone of their conversation turned serious. They sounded like lawyers, informing me time did not matter anymore, they would make my dreams come true from here on out. Further they believed in me and had the financial means to get me everything that I deserved.

There was ten minutes to pass until my departure. I was feeling nauseated and confused. I thought maybe the ice cream the girl used to make the shake was old - wintertime was not the season for cold drinks.

The men's voices softened again as they told me they would start by getting me the boots I had been admiring earlier. They instructed me to turn and take notice of the high-class car they had waiting across the street, inviting me to go in it with them to the shoe store. I could feel my heart beating doubly deep. It was pounding straight into my brain – all at once I was parched, but leery of the milkshake. As I twisted myself around to get a look at the car it hit me they must have seen me in the shoe store earlier.

A familiar feeling swept over me (I called it the *heavy load*) - drugs and heartbreak had triggered this feeling in the past. Also at times it just happened and I never knew why. The heavy load left me feeling as large and weighty as a dump truck. It slowed my surroundings and my heartbeat, making everything gear down almost to a halt.

Slick told me to look in my pocket, so I would see they had already started supporting me. He said we just needed to get in the car together, make a quick stop at the shoe store and then we could head to my new life. I pulled the paper out of my pocket, opened it on my lap, and to my surprise discovered it was a large denomination of foreign money. I quickly jammed it back in my pocket. He leaned into me saying softly he would take me out of the country where I would be free from worry, nobody would know me, and I could get the fresh start I deserved.

His words were almost indecipherable over the ticking of the second hand on the clock. The noise twanged through me, vibrating my insides. There were five minutes before my bus departed. Beads of sweat were dropping off my entire body and even my feet were saturated. I was worried I might be too weak to walk to my bus. If I missed the bus there was no other one until the next day.

Then you briefly appeared - a middle-aged exceedingly petite brunette female with wild short curls, and tiny warm hands. I could not physically identify you or give a sketch artist enough details to compose a picture of you, yet you put yourself in harm's way to help me.

As you marched directly up to me, the man I thought of as One headed outside. You placed a piece of paper in my hand, strolled away stating you would talk to me later. I opened the note on my lap: it contained a phone number along with the words 'I Do Not Trust These Guys If You Need Help Call!'

When Slick spotted you his potent smile transformed into a powerful snarl. He wanted to see the note, wanted me to get in the car right away, and made it clear I owed him, considering the large sum of money he gave me.

The *heavy load* was still weighing on me. I was afraid I might not be able to walk to the exit area. I desperately wanted to be back at the hospital so I pocketed the note, passed the money under the table to Slick and willed myself to stand up. To my relief Slick headed out the front door.

Hollowed and fatigued I shuffled, sluggishly, clutching my bag - the bus was loading as I reached it. I was eager to sleep in my seat and anxious to be at the end of the boarding line.

As I placed my bag into the luggage compartment, passed my ticket to the driver and prepared to ascend the steps of the bus, Slick and three other menacing looking men surrounded me. Slick spoke in a poised and polished manner. He articulated I should be going with him. He stated that I owed it to myself and his friends would never forget what I looked like or where I was from. He rolled and rotated his head towards the three men and then in the direction of the car (which was only a few feet away) letting me know it was running and waiting for us.

An adrenaline rush blasted through me blowing off the *heavy load*. I was trembling. Every bit of my one hundred and fifteen pound being was revved-up. I looked to the driver for help, only to find him visibly shaken; he jumped into his seat, yet left the door open. I crouched into a ball, rolled and bounced myself in between the men on to the top step of the bus. The driver slammed the door shut, and pulled the bus away.

I was wide-awake during the trip back, disgusted and angry with the bus driver, thinking him a coward for not telling the men off. Hours later when I left the bus, I threw the note you had given me at the driver.

Looking back I realize how extremely immature, vulnerable and irresponsible I was to share details of my life with a stranger, and to expect the bus driver to rescue me.

If you had not become involved I might have ended up as just another piece of foreign merchandise. My limited future would have been as a money-making chattel, transported out of the country, with a shelf life expectancy of two years.

You are my beloved tiny female soldier. Thank you for engaging in an age-old battle, and for personally steering me away from danger.

Yours in Feminine Freedom

Love Joie

#36 Study Questions

Food for Thought

1. In what paragraph does Joie realize she is in a dangerous situation? In what paragraph do you detect the probability of danger?

2. Why do you think Joie was targeted by the man she dubbed One – the lure man?

3. What comes to mind when you hear the word recruiter?

Matters of the Heart

1. Discuss incidents of human trafficking in your community.

2. Write a biography on the Tiny Soldier. Be sure to include a detailed physical description.

3. In paragraph seventeen Joie speaks of a familiar feeling she referred to as the 'the heavy load.' Paraphrase this paragraph. Share what your 'heavy load' is. What triggers your 'heavy load?'

#37. Pendulum

This is a love letter, not a romantic one, none-the-less a love letter.

I was relieved your passing would be pain free, yet your terminal diagnosis was unexpected. You were always full of vigour, having been a dedicated worker, and a person who enjoyed travelling. As childish as it seemed, I had the impression you were virtually indestructible - I always assumed you would live out a very long and active life.

I know you did not want to go, you had intended to spend many more moons here with everyone. I also understood you would have preferred him to be the one to care for you, for him to be the one by your side. I did my very best to tend to you, to bring you as much comfort as possible.

The team at the palliative care wing worked with great skill and efficiency. The nicest thing was the unit was quiet, because although you were not in pain, you were sensitive to noise. The room was large and equipped for double occupancy. I was pleased you were the only patient there.

When we first moved to the unit, you enjoyed the view, with your bed beside a large window overlooking a fine garden. In the center of the garden was a gigantic and majestic Maple tree. We speculated as to the age of the tree (you sent me to stand beside it to make a size comparison) concluding it had been here long before either one of us and it would likely remain long after we were gone. During the first day in the room a therapy dog paid you a visit. The friendly Chocolate Lab brought out your bright smile and your girlish giggle. I was happy to see you beam, yet my joy quickly soured, and I had to go sit in one of the quiet rooms and bawl.

I do not remember how many sunrises and sunsets we enjoyed there before I thought it might be our final night together. The rhythm of your breathing had slowed, you had kept your eyes closed and not uttered a sound for a few days. When I roused from my cot that morning, I began to gather your belongings letting you know I was tiding up the room as company was expected.

While your visitors were there I brought your things down to my car, as I moved I heard my own voice mumbling reassurances and guidance. On the way back to your room I remembered that sometime in the night, your breathing had stopped for a few moments, to return in the form of short audible gasps, and your fingers twisted as if to grip a steering wheel.

When your guests left I felt trapped, as if the garden, the room, and the two of us were inside the tip of a pendulum. It was slowly swaying in sync with your breathing - to double time, ta, mm, ta, mm. In an attempt to steady the sway, I held on tight to the rail of your bed with my left hand and adjusted your blankets with my right. It was then I noticed your feet had begun to curl, as if you were a gymnast working on the uneven bars.

I released the blankets and took your hand in mine, bending my knees and leaning my thighs against your bed to balance myself. When I began to caress your head, your chest rose high off the bed and the rhythm of your breathing took a different count - one deep taa, followed by four beats of silence, ending with three short mm, mm, mm. I felt even more cornered as the swaying sensation shifted to move in perfect unison with your breath. The pendulum rocked to the far left and suspended there for four seconds before rocking back and bouncing three times. This movement made it very difficult for me to stand, as I had either no footing or was rebounding.

I struggled to stay stable. An electric-like force engulfed us - it broke the tip of the pendulum, and separated us from the garden.

Although I was relieved the movement had stopped, I was anxious because the unknown energy was gaining momentum and emitting a distinct odour. This stench was similar to when lightning had struck my house years prior. Although I had only inhaled it once, its uniqueness was unforgettable. I hoped the exaggerated charred smell would not linger in my system for months on end as it had before. Along with the odour, the power sent a frenzy of pins and needles rushing over me.

You stopped breathing all together for a time and the electric-like energy centred itself at the tip of my head. When your breath returned the strange power spread all over me again, running willy-nilly.

I had never heard my voice as thick with compassion as when I heard myself speak to you then. Telling you I was sorry he could not be here now and he would not be able to make it in time. I uttered you had done an excellent job, and I thought you should let go.

Just then your last exhale released. I let go of your hand, and a quiet comfort replaced the electric-like force. I felt as hearty and versatile as the majestic Maple. I knew my essence was a miniscule part of a vast universe, and every soul was a piece of an infinite puzzle. I understood your soul had just transformed to fit in elsewhere.

The room and the garden began to shimmer, like dew reflecting the sun, and the glow instantly altered into a dazzling white light. It illuminated with a paranormal brilliance, making everything disappear.

My body felt vacant, and I was void of my natural senses, yet unafraid.

As quickly as the light appeared, it began to thin out as if there was a giant rolling pin smoothing it down. It formed into a thin lightning-like stream, (my natural senses returned) and the stream of light surged penetrating into the crown of my head.

I shouted out that you had died! Even though we were in the palliative care unit, and we had known of your terminal diagnosis for months I was utterly astonished that you had died.

I have only spoken of this incident with four other people. One of them claimed whether real or imagined it was my experience. The others believed it was your final gift to me - a spiritual present for me to treasure...

Yours,

Joie

#37. Study Questions

Food for Thought

1. Research the Maple tree considering:
   (a) its life span
   (b) the average size and rate of growth
   (c) its root formation
   (d) its symbolism in Canadian culture as well as in this Letter.

Matters of the Heart

1. Share how you feel about what Joie described happened to her and the woman inside the tip of the pendulum?

2. Write a paragraph including the words and phrases: electric-like force, unforgettable, distinct odour, paranormal brilliance, dazzling, crown of my head and illuminated.

#38. Tea Box

This is a love letter, not a romantic one, none-the-less a love letter.

Some folks would classify you as an inanimate object, even though you are made of white oak which was once full of life. I do not find it peculiar that I love you. You sit in plain sight a-top my chest freezer in the kitchen where you house my tea. There are always several varieties stored within your five rectangular shaped compartments and your five square sections; bags of green, black, and English breakfast and a variety of loose-leaf flavoured decaf-green.

I do not know who created you or the purpose they had in mind when they designed you to be twenty inches long, twelve inches wide and six inches high. Your thin lid slides out of the grooves that are etched into you length-wise, while a small gold coloured, circular broken lock highlights your front. A few days after I took possession of you I slowly and carefully cleaned you, using lemon oil to bring out a healthy shine in your grains. Every day since, I open you several times a day.

I claimed you as my own the day of my photo finding mission. My first born (the light of my heart and the start of my life) left behind some things at a residence before attending a medical detoxification centre. I agreed to enter the place and retrieve what I could, my main goal was to salvage a collection of family photos.

Over the course of a few days, I knocked on the door of the house several times, each time getting no response, yet I saw three, sometimes four sets of eyes peering at me between a slit in the makeshift curtain. Surmising they were paranoid, unable to open the door, I left a note, letting them know I meant no harm - I simply wanted the pictures.

Later the note was gone but they still would not open the door, so I waited near the walkway close to the place eager to encounter one of the residents. I met up with a young man who was staying at the house, we agreed I could pick up the pictures and any other related items the next afternoon.

The next day as I stepped near the door it swung open, and a shaky yet loud female voice yelled out announcing my arrival. The man with whom I had arranged the meeting bellowed down from the upper level of the house, 'Okay - tell her I will give her the pictures in a minute.' I took a small step inside and was assaulted by a nauseating stench – a mixture of a metallic bitter-sweet smoke and old urine scent.

After catching a quick glance up the staircase and around the living room, I wondered if movie makers had ever been inside a legitimate low-budget drug house, since any movie I watched did not denote a realistic reproduction of one.

The place was in a state of drug-induced disarray. A grayish smog of old smoke drizzled from a few feet below the ceiling. Dried and fresh blood droplets marked the sides of the stairs and the perimeter of the living room. The baseboards were hanging loose or all together removed, and the carpet curled up away from the edges of the room. I could hear the breath of two people coming from the door behind me. I assumed their fingertips were marred from pulling apart the trim and peeling the carpet back. I concluded it would be in my best interest to remain completely still, so as not to upset them.

Several old sun faded sheets covered the glass patio doors, and a heap of wood that likely used to be a rocking chair sat in the corner. The couch, when new, would have been a beige, three cushioned, comfortable place to sit. It was a filthy, brownish dilapidated piece of furniture. It sat on a slant, missing two legs, and instead of a middle cushion, springs protruded. The dirt-caked carpet was mostly black, except for one worn down streak, the legendary *pacing-strip* - the spot where a twitchy person consistently paces. There had been some extensive pacing done on this spot. The strip was worn straight through the carpet and the under padding, buffing the plywood into a smooth shiny surface.

The bones of a coffee table were in front of the couch, four wooden legs, two side rails, and empty groves where the glass top once would have sat. Typical drug house items sat centred in a strikingly straight line under the table: a glass salad bowl full of cigarette butts, a black ashtray with a small heap of ashes in it, a stubby white candlestick and two charred, bent spoons.

The sound of smashing glass rang out, clanging down the stairs, and the breath of the people behind the door became heavier. I fought off the urge to run away. I was going to yell upstairs to ask him if he had the pictures just as he shouted out that he intended to bring them down in a minute.

A pillowcase full of unknown items flew from beyond the landing and fell at the top of the L-shaped stairs. I heard the man step down a few stairs and saw him gently place two more bulging pillowcases on the landing. He disappeared and again the clatter of shattering glass rolled down the stairs. A few minutes passed that way. I could feel perspiration trickling down my sides, but I resolved to stick it out for a while more. I was hoping he would produce the photos soon.

He eventually came down the stairs, clutching the box of pictures to his chest and presented them to me after enacting a deep bow. I responded to his bow with a heartfelt head nod. He instructed me to stay exactly where I was, stating he would bring me everything. An encore of smashing glass resounded before he jumped down the stairs with you, my tea box, in tow.

This time he sported a cynical smirk as he relinquished you to me. It was impossible for me to not cry when I saw you. I was fascinated with you previously, but I did not think I would ever possess you, let alone have the opportunity to put new life into you. He let me know I could go out to put you and the photos in the car, and he would bring out the pillowcases while I did so.

An audible sigh of liberation escaped me as I placed you and the photos in the trunk. I had to stop and take several deep breaths to fill me with the courage I needed to walk back in and retrieve the remaining items. To my delight and intense relief, the pillowcases were sitting on the stoop and the door was closed when I returned.

I was excited to get you home, examine you, clean you out and decide how I was going to use you. First, I sorted through the contents of the pillowcases by slowly dumping their contents onto a sheet I had laid out on the floor. There was nothing in them related to the photos, just random rubbish.

I wiped each photo clean of gritty particles - it was a tedious and sentimental undertaking. I was too exhausted to search through you, so I decided to leave you on the counter until I felt ready to clean you.

A few days later with gloved hands, I slowly slid your thin lid out of its grove. I saw exactly what I expected inside you; the universal paraphernalia of an intravenous drug user. My belly boiled and I upchucked - an intense physiological response to the vision of my child's *gear*. I mopped up, rinsed my mouth, brushed my teeth, showered, changed into fresh clothes, and then I safely and responsibly disposed of your contents.

Every one of my guests has commented on your unique beauty, and my regular visitors enjoy exploring your contents choosing the tasty tea we will share.

Joie

#38. Study Questions

Food for Thought

1. Research death rates and health risks amongst intravenous drug users.

2. What do you consider would be typical items to be found in a drug house?

Matters of the Heart

1. Is there an inanimate object in your home which is of sentimental importance to you? And why?

2. Joie shared she had an intense physiological reaction where her 'belly boiled' and she 'upchucked.' Share an instance where you had a strong physiological reaction.

#39. The Coop

This is a love letter, not a romantic one, none-the-less a love letter.

I thought this letter would have been one of my first, since it was all of you who taught me about love. The three of you helped me to comprehend the highs and lows of love, its many faces, and that it is never static. Yet I believe it is due to my bottomless love for you that this letter has been difficult to write, for agony always accompanies ecstasy. The higher the human heart rises the deeper it drops, and you three have elevated my heart to heavenly heights.

At first, I found love is literally limitless, as it required me to be on duty twenty four hours a day. I needed to be alert and keen, always tending to our nest, trying to sway its every ebb and flow for safety sake - those were such tender and terrifying moments.

Then, the most delightful and physically exhausting time of loving you arrived, the years I was required to formally teach and protect. Surely everyone must live somewhat vicariously while carrying out these responsibilities. With every one of your triumphs, I gleamed and I mourned along with you during all your heartaches. I cherished story time and cried with wonderment as each of you began your journey of reading. It was enthralling to witness the development of your fine motor skills, especially when you conquered tying your own shoes. I am not a cyclist, yet I performed a celebratory dance as each of you took off balancing on two wheels. It was painful when I had to allow you to cross the street on your own. I was beginning to understand that love is often a decision, and at times a particularly painful one. I enjoyed you having your friends visit and am grateful our home was a place where other children wanted to be. Letting you stay with others was awfully tough. I relented though, realizing that love had to take risks, it would be wrong for me to try keep it in a vacuum.

I thrived while preparing for each holiday, the birthday parties, Halloween, Easter, Thanksgiving, Christmas and New Year celebrations were wonderful for me. I found that love was selfless - it gave me peace and a type of tranquility I had never known.

When one of you was permanently absent from our dinner table, love became tumultuous and troublesome. It demanded my surrender - the white flag I had to wave was oversized and cumbersome. Love had the last word. I had to relinquish my leading role and trade it for a spectator's seat up in the bleeders.

Love was a gargantuan grievance for me when you all flew the coop. Even though I knew the three of you were on loan to me, that knowledge did not aid me in my grief. I had to move through it and establish myself anew on the other side of grief.

Now I am reasonably acquainted with my new role, most times I find it especially pleasing. My love for each of you has not faltered but rather its circumference continuously increases.

Having us all together at the dinner table is and will likely always be one of my favourite things. Your shiny faces rejuvenate me and you bring everything that love embodies to the table. My appreciation for the three of you is not a feeling that language could adequately express. Yet I will say, wow, you gave me all that love can give.

Thank you, thank you, thank you...

With all that love can give,

Joie

#39. Study Questions

Food for Thought

1. Discuss the Empty Nest Syndrome.

2. What are some of the many faces of love Joie writes about in this Letter?

3. Paraphrase 'With all that love can give.'

Matters of the Heart

1. Joie stated that 'agony always accompanies ecstasy.' Do you agree with this statement? Why or why not?

2. Who elevated your heart to heavenly heights? And why?

#40. Foreign Territory

This is a love letter, not a romantic one, none-the-less a love letter.

Your sister called me at 8:00 that morning to tell me we had lost you at 5:15. She also wanted me to know I was the brightest light in your life and that you were very proud of me. The tone of her voice dripped with respect. That sentiment gave me the physical strength I needed not to faint, for when I heard you were gone, I quivered, as a lone blade of grass in a strong wind. I knew my existence was going to quake.

When I was a young teenager plotting my way through a hard-hitting subculture, you passed me a pair of shoes. Along with covering my feet, they were an invitation to a new way of living. I was not ready to give-it-a-go then, but three years later, when I was, you were there, with a welcoming smile and outstretched arms. You demonstrated the power and purity of love and bestowed it upon me when I was ignorant. You had an abundance of patience and took pleasure in my company even when I could not bear the feel of my skin. You did everything to help me then, your stamina, beauty and patience were saintly. I used to wonder if in fact you were an alien being, as surely human beings were not capable of such selflessness.

Integrating into the mainstream was tough, and when I had soul-quakes, you would find me hanging by my hair in the aftermath, and help me to free myself, to stand up, carry on and rebuild. Your death is a multiple fracture-my-world-type-of-quake. The terrain of my life is a muddled mess that will not smooth out; instead, I have to find a way to manoeuvre around in it.

I had sincerely encouraged you to let go when I attended your bedside a few days before you died, but upon hearing the news, I changed my mind. I wanted you back. The mature and reasonable part of me is happy for you, as I know your body was tired and the past year was especially difficult. I also realize that you looked forward to the next act, and your absence only seems finite in this realm.

I do not feel mature and reasonable though. You are foremost in my thoughts, and I am hurting like a hungry newborn, ravenous yet unable to feed myself. It has been a few weeks now, the disbelief is starting to wear thin and I find myself wholly heartbroken.

When I wake, I expect to talk with you, and when I remember that we will not physically hear each other it stings, as if billions of miniature blacksmiths are using my body as their forge. I know you cannot come back, but I need to sense that you are okay in your new place, that this change has not separated us.

On the way to your funeral, the others caught sight of two rainbows opposite each other, mirror images. As they were admiring them, an arch of bright-multicolored light sprang out through the middle of one of them and shot off like a shooting star. To my dismay, I could not see them. The others took pictures but the cell phone images were not clear. As they were admiring the rainbows, I recalled how during the freedom ceremony performed at the site of our friend's murder, a triple rainbow had appeared. It was considered a clear message - his spirit was free and would move on. I wondered if I could not see the two rainbows, as I was not ready to accept their symbolism - for most of my life I did attempt to mirror you, and you, my sparkling star, had died.

After your funeral, I sat centred on my living room floor surrounded by articles of yours, the gifts your daughter had given me. I plucked sage from my medicine bag (the one you gave me during our last visit), and performed a smudge, yet I did not feel cleansed. The many items scattered throughout my house you gave to me over the years were no longer a comfort. The furniture, pictures and knickknacks feel like slivers of wood in my fingertips. At times, I find myself entranced and immobilized before them, fighting off the urge to smash them to smithereens.

I still find it hard to accept you have died. I want to check in with you, ask about your day, and let you know the progress of our work. I wish we could laugh and have a dance - I want to continue being your lipstick supplier.

Your sister left me a message before she headed home after the service. She wanted to give me her number and let me know she was concerned for me. This time the tone of her voice denoted a paste-like mixture of grief and love. I played the message several times in order to write it down. She wanted me to know she was sincerely thankful for the real difference I had made in your life. She declared how she was witness to our love and I was the person you felt unconditionally loved by.

I sigh audibly and inwardly when I think of her words, a strange and sad smile slides over my jaw, for you loved me when I knew nothing of love.

Over and Out For Now.

Love Joie

#40. Study Questions

Matters of the Heart

1. How and why can the tone and sentiment in a person's voice give another the strength not to faint?

2. Joie shares that when she remembers her friend is dead 'it stings as if billions of miniature blacksmiths are using her body as their forge.' Can you empathize with her pain? Share your experience with this type of pain.

#41. Mask of Static

This is a love letter, not a romantic one, none-the-less a love letter.

When I spotted you that spring afternoon hanging out at the corner, I wanted to bring you to my place, give you a home. From a block away I suspected you were born sore, I saw it in your stance - posture that portrays nastiness, the type of toughness taught at the school of hard knocks. As I got closer, your attire confirmed my notion, you wore your *new to you* brand name clothes with pride - even though they were a tad too small, stained and threadbare.

The instant I looked at you, I saw the slideshow of your life in your eyes, a tragic tale, with a longing for love its underlying theme. My love for you launched in that moment. I am sorry I was not in the position to give you a home.

If I could have, I would have shared nourishing meals with you and showed you how to keep a joyful house. I wanted to give you happy holidays and help you through school. If I could have, I would have given you the chance to know there is clean love and that your might, channeled right, could bring you positive rewards. I wanted you to believe that not all people *work* each other, and that you could break the cuffs you had inherited.

I had a back seat role in your life, giving you the odd meal and a ride here and there. As spring turned to summer, you were homeless for the first time. I was terrified for you. I did not want the street to hold you in its bowels and churn you into what our society deems a *waste*. We bonded that summer, but it was tortuous for me not to be able to compete with the street phenomenon. I did not have the keys to your cuffs, or the means of plucking you out and placing you somewhere safe.

I had the use of a few different vehicles that summer and it seemed that every time I headed out I would spot you. Each time I picked you up, as you buckled up, your tears fell like a torrent. When you were in that state it brought back memories of my street time. I mourned for the loss of both of our childhoods, and was humbled you felt secure enough in my presence to let go.

At the end of that summer, while I was out walking, I ran into you moments after you were released from your first night in *lock down*. I took that time to speak frankly with you, recanting my recollections of the *drunk tanks*, of how I dried out and straightened out. I let you know I understood what was happening to you, that it could stop now, and I believed you to be worthy and capable of a different way of life. I had nothing tangible to offer you though, and I feared the damage you would sustain in the arms of the correctional system.

When we parted that day, I wanted our hug to transcend the physical realm of touch - to instill in your heart my love, my mindset, and my ever eager willingness to do the next right thing. Our embrace was not a magical change-your-personality-forever-type-of-moment. I held you in my arms briefly, leaned back on my heels to look into your eyes. They reflected a fiery mask of static; the heat was preventing us from truly seeing each other. So I caressed your face, and with the utmost sincerity, I asked you to remember that I loved you.

Over the next while our connections continued. When you would be in the forefront of my thoughts I would encounter you fresh out of *lock down*. I was upset as the penal system seemed to be throwing you at me, but I had no means of catching you. It was clear to me you were at risk and I had serious concerns for your overall health.

Weeks later when a court officer called and asked me if I knew you, iciness took hold of me, as if I were freshly picked produce undergoing the flash freeze process. I thought I was going to be asked to identify your corpse. The iciness melted into scalding disappointment when he put you on the phone - I could not do what you asked of me, and I knew you would be furious with me for not obliging you. The worst part was I could tell that your health had rapidly declined since I had last seen you.

You were then absent for a long time and it pained me that the best scenario I could imagine was you were an inmate. As usual when thoughts of you wore on me like a tight cap, you appeared. I noticed you moments after you stepped off the bus. I was aware you walked inside a pair of shoes commonly issued by our correctional system. To most folks you probably presented as a health buff, a tidy body builder type, but I was fretting for you more than ever. Your new swagger alarmed me; our Provincial Government had branded you with a *jailhouse strut*.

We did not use verbal language or touch to communicate that day, yet a fleeting look spoke volumes to me. I stayed clear of you and consoled myself by believing your subconscious mind would remind you of my fondness for you.

After another long absence from you, I was delightfully surprised when your voice rang out with clarity and assuredness from across the park, and I was warmed by your gentle but secure embrace. That day I learned your childlike hunger for love had progressed into parental passion, and in fact, you were a parent of three youngsters.

You were proud to have me meet them. I was ecstatic; you appeared healthier than I had ever seen you. You glowed with satisfaction as you shared about your job, that you were practically out of the *game*, and that instead you played by your own rules now. Joy pressed warm tears out my eyes when you shared how you were committed to ensuring your children would know a different childhood than yours. You put my number in your phone and we agreed to meet up again soon. As we took leave of each other I noticed newness in your eyes, a simple Innocence seeped out of them. I was refreshed and relieved to see you looking so healthy. I called shortly after seeing you, and during our short conversation, I heard that familiar sense of distress in your voice. I comforted myself knowing that you had my number - you always had a way with numbers.

It was many months before I saw you again. As in the past when I ached with concern for you – presto, you appeared. You were manoeuvring a stroller that contained your youngest child along a flat sidewalk, yet your gait was of a man pushing a boulder-filled wheel barrel up a steep grade. When you noticed me, an eruption of that familiar torrent of tears escaped you - we hugged long and strong affirming our love for each other. I could not assist you as I wanted to, but was able to have you and the baby over a few days later to commemorate your twenty-first birthday. As the celebration ended we vowed to make it an annual tradition.

That was a few years ago, and it is the only birthday dinner I was able to give you. Our last meeting was definitely the most distressing of all for me. You had called to ask a favour of me, which again I was unable to provide but instead you did something for me. I was thankful for your help, yet that hour we spent together haunts me - you were vacant, as though your soul had taken leave of your body. The gray tone of your skin told me of your likely imminent premature death, and it insulated you from me, leaving us detached.

Even though I embraced you, placed our hands together, put my hands on your face, caused our eyes to meet, talked with you and fed you, I was not communing with you. If you are reading, this believe me when I say - I love you, you are good, you are smart, you are skilled and you can break the cuffs of your childhood!

Love Joie

P.S. My number is still the same.

#41. Study Questions

Food for Thought

1. Discuss 'homelessness' within the area you live, the major city closest to you and a city in another continent, considering:
    - (a) contributing risk factors to onset of homelessness
    - (b) rates and age range of homeless people
    - (c) contributing factors to extended periods of homelessness.

Matters of the Heart

1. What does a *wasted* life look like to you and why?

2. Does the memory of an hour you shared with someone haunt you? Explain.

#42. Keep On Knocking

This is a love letter, not a romantic one, none-the-less a love letter.

You certainly were a devoted father. Every Wednesday you were there to see your boys and every weekend they were off with you. I do not think I ever spoke with you - our communication consisted of silent greetings, smiles, head nods and waves.

That is in part why I feel strange writing to you - also I cannot empathize with you but I can merely let you know I wonder about you, and wish you well. What happened to you was beyond me then. I thought those types of occurrences were fictional; soap opera type stories. I moved to the other side of town after your ordeal. Living across the street from that house was deeply distressing. I cannot imagine the depth of your sorrow or the gravity of your loss, and I have no consoling words to offer you.

I found your sons to be adorable little boys - at three and four they knew their Daddy came to see them mid- week, and they looked forward to their weekends with you. I only had a few visits with them – our children had fun together, while I had teatime with the mother of your sons. It was pleasing to have a neighbour with whom I could be cordial, and I thought there was a possibility we could develop a friendship.

One Saturday afternoon while I was having tea across the road, cultish conviction came knocking on the door. It appeared in the form of two young handsome men, dressed in suits and ties. The mother of the house invited them in and asked them to join us. Upon their arrival I left. When they had arrived at my house a few days earlier, I had asked them to stay clear of my door, asserting I had no interest in talking to them.

I arranged to visit your family a few days later, and while the kids were playing I took the time to share that I was taught to respect all manners of religion, that it need not come recruiting, it should attract people on its own, not have to be peddled. The mother of your boys let me know talking to them had been fun and she was really just humouring them.

After their initial visit, I saw those same young men across the street every Wednesday, Saturday and Sunday. A few weeks passed this way and when I tried to arrange a play date for the kids I was told your boys were now being home schooled, and they would only be playing with children of other like-minded parents. I was invited to learn the true way of life. It was made clear to me if I did not embrace their way of living my family and I would no longer be acceptable companions.

I asked her about you then, reminding her you had parental rights and that you may not want this life for your sons. She asserted her boys were in their tender years, that her influence had the most impact at this stage in their lives.

She let me know she was choosing to be involved with the most powerful and righteous group of people who existed. She claimed no individual could compete with this group and also she believed you would chose to get on board rather than have her and the boys move.

She maintained that even though it was an idle threat, she was convinced you would conform rather than risk having her and the boys going to our sister country to live. She shared about the inclusive community awaiting them, that it was capable of providing for all their needs and protecting them against non-believers.

I truly trusted that her claim was an empty threat, for I could not fathom why a mother would consider taking her sons away from a dutiful and devoted Father.

Not too long after that conversation everyone on the street discovered your boys and their Mother had vanished.

Humans place themselves at the top of the food chain, considering themselves to be the highest of all mammals. From that superior spot we demonstrate the widest range of heinous behaviours. Time has taught me these types of atrocities are commonplace, yet as a bystander I find them impossible to digest.

Thinking of You,

Joie

#42. Study Questions

Food for Thought

1. In your own words define:
    (a)   'cultish conviction'
    (b)   solicitation
    (c)   kidnapping.

Matters of the Heart

1. This Letter was written when the boys were in their tender years. Write three follow-up Letters (twenty years later) one to the father, one to the mother and one to the boys.

2. Discuss 'Humans place themselves at the top of the food chain, considering themselves to be the highest of all mammals. From that superior spot we demonstrate the widest range of heinous behaviours.'

#43. Coagulation

This is a love letter, not a romantic one, none-the-less a love letter.

I struck gold when you entered my life, not the kind that the pawnshop owners thrive on, rather a spiritual gold. Thank you for bonding with me, (for staying stuck) and for sharing the hilarious memory of your cologne incident.

Prior to the day you *gold dusted* me we had only interacted a few short times. It was an action-packed time and you were the newbie of the group. I found you to be handsome, impeccably dressed and well mannered - the naive boy from the cologne test long since coagulated into you. The general consensus was that you were by far the coolest of us all, and we would be fortunate to have you in our clan.

When I saw you approaching me that day, I wanted to hold you in conversation, longing for your acceptance and approval. Your accent captivated me and your gaze was spellbinding – it inundated me with an unknown energy, leaving me motionless.

Your eyes were fixed on mine, yet you looked through me, from somewhere beyond the realm of the human eye. The gaze was sweetly and gently interrogating, rendering me raw yet undisturbed.

A heavenly sensation of pins and needles paraded over me, filtering in through my third eye, and dusting down into my wounded soul. I was speechless, my tongue thick with tranquility. As your gaze shifted back to the physical realm, the dust settled, coagulating. I stood astonished before you.

The gold dusting was our bonding moment, a rare flash of authentic empathy - two souls engaged and a strand of each entwined. You only spoke ten words to me during our exchange. I did not utter a word, yet the communication was commanding.

You used your experience (a sprinkle of your gold dust) and your strong Alpha sensibilities to lift my loneliness, imprinting me with the know-how to sit in solace. Thank you for initiating our relationship and for repeatedly telling me 'Baby Girl, all you got to do is call, twenty fourrr hours a day, sevennn days a week, three hundred and sixty fiveee days a year!'

I was enjoying my second visit with you in your Town, when you shared your hilarious account of the cologne incident. We lived at opposite ends of the Continent, and I was still a baby when the big machine of advertising worked its magic on you, hooking your tween-aged brain. You would not rest until you had the cologne for yourself, to put it to the test.

You acquired the bottle and for the first time your whole being bubbled over with anticipation, for you knew from here on out you were going to be a babe-magnet. After liberally dousing yourself with the magical liquid, you flexed your triceps and took a deep breath readying yourself for the big moment. A flame of fear scorched you, knowing that momentarily you would be knocked to the ground by a band of beauties, but you did not relent.

You headed out and after taking a few steps, aggressively shut your eyes and squeezed your body tightly, conscious that the women would want to feel your burly muscles. You stood strong and motionless for what seemed like years - much to your dismay no one touched you.

You opened your eyes to face your first sting of romantic heartbreak. It was a vehemently vicious slap - there was not even one gorgeous female in sight. At your tender age you feared there was a fundamental flaw in you for surely the cologne was not to blame. It was a spirit-crushing blow.

Not too long after, you reached the age of reason and understood advertising is a lure, and in your innocence it took you in hook, line and sinker.

For me, life is love, and love entails each moment and the entire gamut of emotions that it may incite. Since we bonded my tendency to be overwhelmed with loneliness has vanished for I know you are in my corner.

With Love and Respect

Joie

#43. Study Questions

Food for Thought

1. Describe how a look can come from somewhere beyond the realm of the human eye.

2. Discuss the power of advertising considering:
   (a)　what makes a successful advertisement?
   (b)　the right and need to advertise?
   (c)　laws governing advertising?

3. What is the symbolic meaning of the title of this Letter?

Matters of the Heart

1. When have you been '*gold dusted*' by someone as Joie was? Share the details of the relationship you have with the person with whom you bonded.

#44. My Reflection

This is a love letter, not a romantic one, none-the-less a love letter.

I loved you more than my own breath then, believing I would die if you went away from me. I thought that in your absence my eyes, ears and nose would turn to stone. Actually, I knew without you every part of me would just jam up, I would become as stiff as rock, and with the slightest touch I would disintegrate. Even then, I knew you did not adore me as I did you. Yet that did not matter to me, as long as I could be near you, I was at ease.

Contentment was lying face-to-face with you, eating your exhales. I did whatever it took to take in your breath, believing it to be the ultimate elixir. Early morning mouth, coffee or cigarettes did not sour the scent of your breath. Anything that came from your body was just some of the icing on the cake that was you.

I was fascinated with your long lanky fingers and legs and astonished by each bump on your spine. Your hair enthralled me. I tried many times to curl each strand through my fingers. It was the softest, dreamiest substance in the world and I wanted to feel every long lock that came out of your scalp.

To nestle in the nape of your neck was a primary goal of mine; while I was there a supernatural force protected me from all harm. Even the slam of a super-hero's hammer could not hurt me in your embrace. Slowly running my fingers around the outline of your u-curved fingernails was an addiction for me, it put me in a hypnotic state - I was completely under your command.

Your eyes held the meatiest magic. When I saw my reflection in the brown golden flecks of them I was in a state of bliss, where I wished to always be. Experience taught me that it was impossible though, you would feel pestered if I persisted on trying to maintain soft gazing eye contact with you. I resigned myself to accept that it was a rarity, which made it even more heavenly when it happened.

When you spoke, each word was a bubble that held me, softly bouncing me on to the next, so at times I had difficulty following your story lines. But that was okay with me, as I could ask you to tell me again - only you told stories that were worth hearing over and over.

The tale of your birth was my favourite! I pictured it as a regal and dramatic scene. You (the most beautiful new-born ever) came into the world on the other side of our Country on a small Isle. This Isle endures some of the harshest weather winter offers. For you to be examined by a proper doctor, you had to travel to the Mainland by sled. You screamed bloody murder the entire trip. Your parents thought you did not like being thickly swaddled, but the doctor discovered there was a diaper pin pinched straight through the flesh on your left hip. It was an accidental puncture. I pulled and probed at the skin and finding no scar, I preferred not to think of the painful part of your story.

Instead, I pictured you as an exotic Princess born on a tiny dazzling snow-covered Isle. You were swathed in the finest of furs and safely secured on a fire-truck red sled to make your first journey to the Mainland. The finest doctor in the Province was elated to examine you, and humbled to have the honour of registering your birth.

I lived for you and through you then, knowing little of my own form or being, my existence bound to you as a skydiver to their parachute.

Yours,

Joie

#44. Study Questions

Food for Thought

1. At what stage of life is it reasonable for a person to love another more than their own breath?

Matters of the Heart

1. Whose voice have you found to be as captivating as Joie described 'each word was a bubble that held me, softly bouncing me on to the next?' And what is the nature of your relationship with this person?

2. When have you lived through someone, 'bound to them as a skydiver to their parachute?' Explain the dynamics of such a relationship.

#45. Pearl Drops

This is a love letter, not a romantic one, none-the-less a love letter.

I do not know your name, your gender, nor when and where you lived. I do know that I have loved you and yearned to find out everything about you for most of my life. From the start of my remembrances I had a feeling you were with me, envisioning you with all my senses. Intuitively I believe you know more of me than anyone, including me. I write to you with an obliging heart and light fingers.

There were two Grand women in my life. I knew they were Grand before I knew what the title represented, or that words were sounds used as part of language. They were Grand because I loved the scent of their bodies and the sound of their voices most of all. I did not get to be with them at the same time, or in the same places, but I delighted in their company especially when I was able to go into their worlds.

These women were the only people I knew who had stockpiles of Pearl Drops inside their eyes - whenever they looked at me the weightless, translucent, sweet smelling Drops came barrelling out. It did not matter what part of me they were looking at, the Drops never failed to fall. I was duty driven to have and horde the Drops. I loved collecting them as much as I loved the Grand women. I would fill my pockets and bags with them, build huge heaps of them, rub them all over me and even eat them.

One of the Grand women had come from beside the Ocean to the City. She made her living in all sorts of ways, drove many different cars, and had a neat, lively vernacular. Some people claimed not to be able to understand her but I grasped every word she said, and could speak just like she did. The Trinity was valid and important to her, as were certain superstitious beliefs. I knew I could not have come from the Ocean, the thought of unending blue water and all its strange sea creatures vexed me, turning my tummy.

The other Grand female was a woman from the place of the Tall Trees. She did not ever move far from her birthplace where she used to travel via horse and buggy and never did take to driving a car. She spoke two languages. I used to be able to understand both of them but could only ever speak one. I tried to twist my tongue to speak her language, only ever imitating a slight hint of it. The Trinity was everything to her providing her with a husband, children and lush land. I could not master her knitting and sewing needles and always got a headache trying to work in the garden.

One time during a stay in the land of the Tall Trees, I became especially frustrated trying to work with wool. Angry tears fell, all my muscles stiffened, and my stomach spun wildly until I threw up. I was disgusted with myself for being a bad helper, and after my belly cooled down I felt flat, like a raw, rolled out pastry. I tried to perk myself up, gathering as many Pearl Drops as I could.

The women of the quilt were there working and as I scurried around scooping up Pearl Drops, I heard one of them whisper dirtily that my fits were a result of my 'Sang Rouge.' It struck me as a peculiar thing to say. I recognized what she meant by the fit - that was my tantrum, but I was baffled by the mention of my red blood. I had seen red blood between my mother's legs but she had reassured me that it had nothing to do with me.

For the first time, the Pearl Drops I collected failed me. I did not rise up, even when I swallowed a whack of them and vigorously rubbed my face and heart area with them. As my visit ended two questions gnawed at me. Was my blood red? What color blood did the women of the quilt have?

Pearl Drops never flowed out of my Grand women after that day.

On the way home I decided to puncture my skin to discover the exact color of my blood. It was difficult to decide what to cut my hand with, and to find the time alone to do it. I heeded the ominous warnings against touching my father's razors and the deadly sharp knives in the house. One day I spotted a paperclip. Thinking it might do the trick, I stashed it in my pocket until I had the chance to see if it would work.

That afternoon, while my mother watched her program, I wiggled on my belly under the trailer that held the winter wood and took out the glittering sliver clip. I felt as mighty as any hard working man when I pulled it open. It took a firm resolve and two tough twists to straighten it out.

As I pinched the clip between my left index finger and thumb, a drop of glittery sweat hit the dirt under me. I extended my palm up as if to offer a dog a treat, then I bent my thumb as close to my palm as it would go. The bend created a small fleshy section of skin - I first lightly grazed it with the tip of the clip. Immediately I was parched. I took the incredible thirst as my prompt to push and scrape the clip as deep and as fast as I could.

There, under the shelter of the winter wood, with the light of the sun's rays ricocheting off the paper clip, one of my questions was satisfied. The whisper of the women of the quilt was true.

Drops of rich, red coloured blood had come out of me, mixing with my sweat in the dirt. In that instance my love for you was conscious and deliberate.

I had *Sang Rouge*.

Always Calling to You

Joie

#45. Study Questions

Food for Thought

1. Who is Joie writing to in this Letter?

2. What is the subject of this Letter?

3. Define *Sang Rouge*.

Matters of the Heart

1. As a child what were your Pearl Drops?

2. Joie stated that 'Pearl Drops never flowed out of my Grand women after that day.' Why did the stockpile of translucent sweet smelling Drops dry up?

#46. Spring Walk

This is a love letter, not a romantic one, none-the-less a love letter.

Another spring has sprung (not with much of a bounce mind you) but the harshest winter in fifty odd years is over and to everyone's relief it took the snow with it. It is the twenty eighth spring to arrive since your departure, and I think of you no less.

The grass is sprouting up around your headstone - it is what you called boogie green, a bright, brilliant lime green. Mourners are visiting the yard more frequently, leaking laughter and tears which call to the names etched on the stones. Without me realizing it, the headstones have multiplied. The marble markers that once stood as thin patches of hair on a scraggly cat are now erected more like carefully stacked dominoes.

I know others visit your gravesite - some of them leave tangible traces of themselves behind: coins, pendants, notes, flowers and other personal mementos. I am not the only one who clears away leaves and scrubs your headstone, yet during my almost sixteen years of visiting, I have never encountered anyone there.

The ending of winter is reminiscent of your walk, your infamous spring-off-the-balls-of-the-feet kind of walk. No matter the speed at which you were moving, each step was like a mad exodus. I brought someone new to the alley to show her your shoeprints in the cement. She deduced you were a sizeable person - I set her straight, letting her know your feet were huge compared to the rest of you. I suppose that is why you had an infamous way of walking.

I have a vivid memory of us wall climbing that day. I was convinced without a doubt we had super powers, we jumped from roof top to roof top and shimmied up and down the alleyways with grace and ease. You intentionally dropped down to leave your mark in the cement.

I am thankful for those shoeprints. Now that spring has washed the winter salt and ice down the gutters, I have a clear view of the markings. I look forward to standing in those newly washed prints every spring. It is a spiritual experience for me, a cleansing of my conscience and a re-start of my heart. Every time I place my feet in your prints I enjoy a vision of you and our youth, of fighting and forgiveness, of grieving and growing; a virtual mishmash of the experiences of my life.

If we were young and able to climb that way today, you would be creating a video on your tiny cell phone, (some as small as my hand) and uploading it to the Internet. In 1989 the Internet started out as the World Wide Web. It was said to be an instantaneous way of recording and retrieving information through computers. Videos can spread faster than Spiderman's thread on this Web. Within seconds, someone on the other side of the world is able to view an upload. I do not claim to grasp it and am uncomfortable with it, yet I have somewhat conformed to the many so called technological advances of the last few decades.

I was taught about the Web from my firstborn, the baby who was developing in my uterus when you died. That was a typical scenario as many of the 'Y' generation (those children born in the 1980's or

1990's) taught their elders the new technology. When my child was in grade one the school informed me that to ensure his education was adequate I needed to provide a computer with Internet access at home.

With this in mind, and knowing my electric typewriter was not going to make the grade for me at college, I purchased a computer for the children and me. If you were still with us I am sure you would be what we call a techie, whereas I am almost technologically illiterate.

I have dubbed the 'Y' generation, the Thumb-Using Generation, on account of how they excessively use their thumbs. To play a video game we needed quarters and an Arcade. Then it was a matter of controlling a joystick and maybe pressing a button, but today people constantly fiddle electronics with their fingers. A new need for fine finger motor dexterity has arisen that has changed human beings. Like any change there are good and bad repercussions - time will tell.

I really wish you were here, and I know even though you would mock me for my ignorance, you would help me cope with this technical world. The extreme use of technology, coupled with a constant intake of junk food, has produced many obese people, and social interactions are completely different from when we were youngsters. The go-to source of communication for lots of people is through the Internet on an entity referred to as Social Media. I am almost half a century old now and am already finding the changes in the world highly strange...

People sit in the same room and communicate through their phones, rather than talking to each other. A great deal of arguing and bullying goes on this way. It is easier for people to be rude when the spewing is silently punched out of their finger tips onto a keypad rather than face-to-face.

Part of why I could not allow myself to grieve over you for so long was that our last conversation was a bitter one. Historically our arguing was fierce and had an infamous reputation. Others learned the rule to abide by regarding our frothy fighting - do not interfere. Our other *partner* was the only person permitted to attempt peacekeeping missions between us. If anyone else tried, our wrath instinctively coupled and we lashed against them. Our brawls were a symptom of our love, and although we were very cruel to each other, in a red-hot minute we would insanely defend each other against any outsider.

The only physical part of our last argument was our collision as we rounded that well known seedy downtown corner. I was aware it was likely our last chance to meet for a long time, but had no inkling it would be our final conversation.

I have a detailed memory of your physical image and your scent from that day. But I cannot conger up a clear sounding remembrance of your voice. Yet I internally recanted the words we exchanged during our last meeting thousands and thousands of times. The cruel tone and the merciless meaning of the words sat in my heart where I held tight every fiery word we exchanged.

Recounting the conversation fourteen years later to my Old Man was a massive emotional purge for me. I told him I was close to a year off the streets and straight as a pin when we collided, that you seemed *fresh out*, and you were definitely *blazing*. As I told him the details of the ferocious argument, my long-held heart-burn boiled over, and a batch of searing grief-filled tears overflowed. He understood the nature of our rare love, and how the sight of you was a potent summons, pleading me back to my old familiar way of life.

After deciphering the details through my bawling, my Old Man applied his logical insight, acted as a go-between and smoothed everything out. So you see my friend, some things never change. Even in your absence the third member of our trio is our arbitrator, the tension dissolver, the ever sound voice of reason. You sure knew what you were doing when you played cupid with us.

We were a tight and terrible trio then. I want you to know even though you are not here in the flesh, we have developed a mature and safe-minded sense of your ingenuity, loyalty and courage. We do have down times, yet we move right through this life as you taught us, never leaving laughter more than a day or two behind.

Your love enhanced me - the virtually unattainable intimacy, the odd tender moment, all the jabbing, and even your premature death, prompted me to stand a little straighter, to stay a little longer and to savour each moment. I give all I can to life - I give of myself and I give for you.

Love Joie

Just a Stupid Girl

#46. Study Questions

Food for Thought

1. What traits are revealed about Joie's red-headed friend in this Letter?

2. Discuss the Y generation taking into consideration:
   (a) what did many of them teach their parents?
   (b) Joie's term the 'Thumb-Using generation.'
   (c) how has new modes of communication influenced and affected day to day life?

Matters of the Heart

1. Do you have a special spot you like to go to meditate or reminisce? Why?

2. Paraphrase the last paragraph of this Letter sharing about someone you loved who has died.

#47. The Plaque

This is a love letter, not a romantic one, none-the-less a love letter.

I want to stand up, as you taught me, not be stagnated by grief. At times I am doing just that, and then something either refreshing or frustrating happens and instinctively I want to call you. I did not realize how much I would miss you. I am not constantly morbid or joyless, but life is consistently awkward without you. Like you eating your weekly hotdog without the ketchup, or like me eating my morning oatmeal without the unsweetened applesauce and cinnamon.

For much of our relationship we were both on the go a great deal so we did not have a lot of time to talk, but the last decade, I mostly worked from home and you were retired. This gave us many opportunities to chat on the phone. The conversations were invaluable and even though our face-to-face visits were few, our bond strengthened.

You told me every day in the last few months of your life how incredibly important I was to you – adamantly asserting 'I really, really, reallyyy, reallyyyy, love you! We are like two peas in a pod, and as thick as thieves.'

I moved last month and yesterday I unpacked the final two boxes. The last item I removed was the plaque with the famous three-lined prayer on it that you gave me in 1985. Grief beckoned me with a bold burning in my belly and a tight constriction in my throat and chest. Panic greeted my grief when I saw that the bottom right hand corner of the logo was peeling off the plaque. As I clutched it tight to my chest attempting to combat my physical discomfort, I noticed your handwriting on the back. When I ran my fingers along your blue-inked etchings, calmness and peace enveloped me as though you were embracing me and telling me you were proud of me.

The comforting feeling started with a balmy tingling that travelled up my fingers and exploded at my wrist, splattering my whole body. In that flash of harmony, I was aware of love's ability to linger - tasting its leftovers with all my senses. For that moment I was not longing or a little off, everything was as it should be.

The calmness quit as quickly as it had arrived when the fire in my throat and my quivering lip reminded me you had died six months ago. I set out with great urgency to repair the logo, weeping when it seemed my attempts to stick it back into place might fail. There was a notion inside me, telling me I would be letting you down if I were unable to keep it intact. To my relief the white sticky gel I applied in between the wood and the paper adhered and held the logo in its original spot.

I do not mind that the corners are chipped and the once deep gold and rust brown colouring has long since faded to a dull orange and dirty brown. It is acceptable to me that I do not remember you presenting it to me, but I cannot stomach the thought of the logo separating from the wood.

Both of our belly button birthdays are this month, and yesterday the girls had a celebratory lunch for me. The little lady that took her spot in our lives a few months back gave me a pretty peach coloured earth-friendly card. The card is adorned with purple tulips and beige and light green decorative swirls. She purchased it for you, but was unable to get it to you before you passed; hence it landed in my lap. I was glad that when you checked her out a few months earlier, she met with your approval, as you declared she was 'Worth keeping!' She eases my grief and motivates me to keep passing along what you taught me.

There is no typical birthday message written on the card, no inscription, instead, just one sentence on the front that reads,

'Light tomorrow with today!'

Over and Out For Now

Love Joie

#47. Study Questions

Food for Thought

1. Joie wrote 'In that flash of harmony, I was aware of love's ability to linger – tasting its leftovers with all my senses.' Consider the following:
   - (a) what is it about love that gives it the power to linger?
   - (b) what does lingering love taste like to you?
   - (c) describe how you experience love with all your senses. Be sure to include your sixth sense.

Matters of the Heart

1. What does the phrase 'Light tomorrow with today' mean to you?

#48. Refuse

This is a love letter, not a romantic one, none-the-less a love letter.

I want you to know I find it distressing that you think poorly of yourself for the problems you were part of so long ago. It saddens me when you get disillusioned with yourself.

Of course, it is always good to keep on keeping on, and to want to do better every day, yet I wish for you to be as accepting of yourself as you are of others. Those times when you get fuming on the exhaust of the world's grime, you search to understand the source, and either contribute to reducing it or find a form of forgiveness for it. It is time to exonerate yourself, exhale the refuse, and take refuge in your gifts.

It is understandable for you to identify with the mixed- up vulnerable little girl you once were, but also accept that is was a time full of wonderment and magical thinking. When you feel a smack from the past reminding you of what a troublemaker you once were, spiritually slap yourself into recalling one of your selfless acts during your almost thirty years of service. When you look at your socio-economic status and see inferiority glaring back, glimpse at your health history and accept that you are fighting a good fight. Even your favourite fictional boxing hero would be proud of you.

You are a beautiful and integral part of the immense universe. The earth is a better place for your presence. Be as forgiving to yourself as you are forgiving of others.

Ever enjoying learning to love you,

Joie

#48. Study Questions

Matters of the Heart

1. How do you define self-love?

2. Joie stated 'It is time to exonerate yourself, exhale the refuse, and take refuge in your gifts.' Consider:
   (a) What do you think are some of the issues Joie needs to exhale?
   (b) What issues do you need to exhale?
   (c) What gifts do you think Joie could take refuge in?
   (d) What gifts can you take refuge in?

3. Write a letter to yourself. Be sure to include the words or phrases: accepting, disillusioned with yourself, exonerate, spiritual slap, wonderment and magical thinking, health history, contribute to reducing it, beautiful and the earth is a better place for your presence.

#49. Glistening Tires

This is a love letter, not a romantic one, none-the-less a love letter.

When I saw you, it was the first time I had laid eyes on a human being who had a purple tinge to their skin. You are the most gigantic man I have ever stood beside. Thank you for pulling over to help me that day. It was long before cell phones were commonplace, so you really did save the day.

I was moving fast on a major highway when I felt the front passenger tire give way. It exploded with a deafening roar and the car pounded forward like a mad dog with a severed right leg. My reflex response was a death grip on the steering wheel, my passenger's usual fair complexion turned green and she let out a glass-shattering screech.

Fate placed a cut off directly in front of me and the car made a few final piercing pounds into the parking lot of a mechanic's yard. It was desolate of human life, but on the right side of the garage was a huge pile of tires. Compared to the mangled remnants of my tire these tires glistened with life.

My passenger jumped out of the car and upchucked as I attempted to release my grip on the steering wheel. Fight for homeostasis made the scene dreamlike - her gagging sounded thunderous, my eyes fixated on the luminous glistening tires. I was attempting to coach my hands to let go of the steering wheel when I intuitively realized there was another presence in the yard.

You had expertly parked your rig partly in the yard and partly leaning toward the ditch. When I saw you descending from the cab I snapped out of the trance I was in, let go of the wheel and got out of the car.

I had spent time with several types of large sportsmen, yet your enormity was spectacular. I was painfully aware of the strain in my neck as I attempted tomake eye contact with you.

Today I believe you had an African accent. Yet it was the first time I had heard words spoken in that manner. Each one started out almost silent and ended with a weighty inflection. You stopped after another trucker radioed, letting you know there were two women in trouble with a blown tire.

I took a tire from the pile and as you proceeded to put it on the car I left a note with my number on it offering payment. Again, thank you for taking time away from your work to stop to help us.

Sincerely,

Joie

#49. Study Questions

Food for Thought

1. Joie mentioned that this incident took place long before cell phones were commonplace. Discuss the pros and cons of cellular phones.

2. Define homeostasis.

3. Describe a scenario when you fought to maintain homeostasis.

Matters of the Heart

1. Compile a comprehensive list of people who have helped you. Remember it is not necessary to have met the people on your list.

#50. Branded

This is a love letter, not a romantic one, none-the-less a love letter.

I am not sure who called and asked me to come, but they said he was in trouble again. Everyone was getting scared - they felt if I could talk to him, maybe we could nip it in the bud. For many reasons nobody wanted it to go full bloom. I was worried he might not survive another episode, so I drove up right away. The doctors were very explicit the last time, informing us his heart could not take much more and that it would likely explode if he got carried away again.

During the three-hour drive up there I attempted to tame my nervousness with music by blaring out the radio - blasting the songs I liked the most and willing my daunting memories to drone away with the fading drumbeats.

The overpowering scents of his illness are always the first of my recollections. His unique true scent was masked with typical bodily excretions, mixed with the after smell of tobacco, alcohol, trees, chainsaws, gas, leather and rubber. If he was still recognizable the familiar and easily delectable whiff of his old school cologne would echo through my heart.

Typically my olfactory memories are closely followed by the absurd audio: a mix of disturbing laughter, loud, odd repetitive sounds, the shrieking of tears born of mammoth grief, along with rapid speech, broken sentences and an eerie dense silence.

The visuals always come to me after the audio. During this ride, I fought firmly against them, turning the music up to keep them from entering my field of vision. I wanted only the view of the highway in my sight. My desire was to drive wisely, arrive safely.

When I pulled into town, it was easy for me to find him and I was pleasantly relieved that he was glad to see me. The grin and glossy eyed glare radiating from his face reinforced my notion that the mania was gathering strength. My retrospect was clear on this matter. I knew if it took siege, psychosis could obtain permanent residency in him. I was desperate to convince him to take his medication.

We sat in my car and I let him know many of us were worried about him. I tenderly reminded him I wanted him with me for a long time, reiterating he needed to keep a safe and steady heart rate so as not to blow it up.

That is when he told me of you, his new girl friend, declaring you were a 'Bona fide beauty pageant world champion type beauty!' I was respectfully skeptical as I listened to his story that not only was he taking his medication, but he got the royal treatment when he did. He claimed for the last while he was receiving preferential treatment at the drug store and thrice daily the staff revered him as a king. He knew this because he did not have to wait in line - everyone moved aside as he approached, and a glass of water with a pill were placed directly into his hand. Also after he ingested them, he was often given a candy. What really made it a regal experience for him was the most beautiful woman in the world was waiting on him.

My skepticism formed a vast lump of anxiety in my larynx that I had to choke down as I considered what he was telling me. We drove to the drug store and he challenged me to 'come to meet the beauty' and to 'witness how a king is treated.'

I waited outside and peered in through the window, for experience had taught me he might believe he is receiving royal treatment but the people he was interacting with may be cautiously guarded.

As I caught sight of what was happening inside the drug store, the sour anxiety I had swallowed transformed into a rare sweetness, and I was gladdened with gratitude. You left your work and came out from behind the counter as soon as you noticed him there. I entered the store and approached close enough to watch what transpired between the two of you.

I saw what a strikingly gorgeous woman you were. Your physical form is a rarity, yet your genuine down-to-earth professional manner was the real rarity. Compassion and open-mindedness encompassed you. I only knew of one other medical professional who treated him with genuine respect.

I stood mesmerized, watching your communication - I could not hear a word the two of you exchanged, yet the pale yellow pigments of pixel-like energy that moved between both of you spoke volumes. It said you were applying your training with the utmost integrity, by treating a man with dignity and treating his illness with the appropriate medication. My spirit heard – 'be refreshed and renewed with optimism.'

I did not approach you then to thank you, feeling we could keep up the fight more effectively if I did not interfere in your relationship with him. Knowing what you were doing was like a gift of the latest-greatest armour that technology had to offer, and for the first time I thought there was only a slim chance his disease would conquer him.

I stayed in town a few nights longer and was successful in getting him to eat, at first only a few bites, but before I departed he had taken in a full meal. I only ever mentioned you once to him. With a wink I stated such a beloved king as himself must always be gentle with his helpers, and only ever greet them inside the drugstore of which he presides. His face flushed red as he let me know he was fortunate to have a friend at the drugstore and he would not do anything to jeopardize that alliance.

His health had a long and strong good spell after you helped him to get a steady intake of his medication. A few years later I was able to move back to his area and spend quality time with him. Aging often complicates pre-existing maladies and although he did have a troublesome time near the end of his life, I am especially pleased to tell you he passed away placidly.

As I sang Amazing Grace at his funeral a reel of fast moving faces flashed though my mind. Yet the image of your face was steady and clear. So I knew I needed to seek you out.

Even through my thick grief it was easy for me to find you. I awkwardly blubbered out a thank you for being kind to him. Soft words of condolence rolled off your tongue and empathy ricocheted out of your eyes as you asked me his name.

Nine years passed before I saw you again. At first glance I failed to recognize you as his friend, but the rare air of quality care you were providing made me look twice. I waited until the next time I saw you to mention him and was tickled-pink to introduce you to his great-grandchild.

Thank you for your exceptional service. The people of our Province are fortunate to have you as a health care provider. Surely your genuine heart-warming brand of professionalism has affected the lives of countless other families, and branded their hearts with optimism.

Sincerely,

Joie

#50. Study Questions

Food for Thought

1. Define mania and psychosis.

2. Discuss mental illness considering:
   (a)   the DSM 5
   (b)   laws governing Mental Health in your place of residence
   (c)   common myths regarding mental illness
   (d)   ECT.

Matters of the Heart

1. Who do you love who has a mental health diagnosis? How does their illness manifest itself in your relationship?

#51. Majestic Constellation

This is a love letter, not a romantic one, none-the-less a love letter.

Sorry I was slow writing this letter, it is not for lack of thinking of you. I hold you in my heart and behind my eyes, wanting to give you the chance to see almost everything I do - you are *gone but not forgotten*.

When I started this letter we had not had much of a winter, being cold enough for snow only a few days at a time. Then the water levels would rapidly rise along with the temperature.

The last several weeks have consisted mostly of a deep freeze, the must-stay-indoors or suffer frostbite in three minutes kind of cold. I only have one remembrance of us on a winter day. It is a fragmented and tired memory yet what remains is crystal clear, as if frozen solid in time.

I was guzzling booze, revelling in the familiar tingling of its heat as it slid down my throat, burning my belly, lighting up my senses - my mind was clear, my body satisfied. Then our infamous trouble making trio was tossed on to the street. We bounced up with the stupefied stamina of bodies drowning in alcohol and headed towards our dug-out.

On our way my sinew thunderously quivered and I was bone tired, so I dropped to the ground. You were livid when you realized I was not keeping up. However, your kicks and slaps were virtually undetectable and your usual spine churning 'Just a Stupid Girl' chant sounded as I imagined an overseas phone call would, distant and hollow.

The last bit of my wintery remembrance is of the pure and peaceful bliss that overtook me when you pulled the wooden plank atop us in our dug-out. The high I was experiencing was a foreign one, smooth and stilling. If the angel of Death had beckoned me I would have placidly pursued. It was your warm bodies against mine and the beating of your hearts that droned a call of survival to me - once again your love insisted that I live.

The evening of your murder we were living in the confines of polar opposite sub-cultures, yet within the same time zone. I was star gazing, softly talking to my unborn child, and caressing my belly around the time you hit the ground. I console myself with the belief we were both admiring our majestic constellation from a similar viewpoint the moment of your passing. It comforts me to know the splendid sight of our sky was in your sight as you travelled to your new destination.

Love Joie

Just a Stupid Girl

#51. Study Questions

Food for Thought

1. What do the homeless people in your area do to cope with extreme weather?

2. Do you know where homeless people in your area store their belongings?

3. Where and how do homeless people in your area obtain food?

Matters of the Heart

1. Paraphrase the last paragraph of this Letter.

2. Joie said 'It comforts me to know the splendid sight of our sky was in your sight you as you travelled to your new destination.' Share a comparable statement you have experienced or that someone you know has experienced.

#52. Subliminal Sausage

This is a love letter, not a romantic one, none-the-less a love letter.

Last week my olfactory bulb released a pent-up reminder of your deathbed. It was a regurgitation of the metallic-like scent that emanated out of your mouth and off your pores during our last visit. The reminders were not triggered by conscious minded memories. The first time it happened, I had finished tidying my bed and was heading down the hallway to make tea, when unexpectedly my glasses fogged (as if I had just come in from the cold), and the scent inundated me. I was unruffled by this occurrence, naturally considering it a celestial visit from you, so I verbally invited its return.

The moments the scent and fog befell me were quiet and profound instances of love that I doubt I will often get to experience. It happened three more times, first while I was pounding the keyboard, then when I was reading and lastly as I was relaxing in front of what you called the 'boob tube.' Each time, as the fog lifted and the scent dissipated, I found myself in the moment of our final physical visit, a bittersweet space to be.

As I bent over your hospital bed, took your left hand in mine and put my face near yours, I tasted the fragrance of your imminent death. I leaned in further, lightly sang into your ear, and declared my undying dedication and love for you. I consciously exhaled into your mouth, releasing my love-filled Co2 into you, expecting it to help you pass smoothly. I filled my lungs with your exhale, wanting to grasp it, to take hold of your spunky sweetness. You were aware of my presence and I felt my affection wholly returned.

We silently communed, saying farewell to our usual way of being. I can purposely ponder on this memory now without evoking tears, yet I miss you none-the-less. I love you none-the-less.

The last several years I have been accustomed to eagerly waking at 5:00am, placing one of my plants on the table and getting to work. Aside from tending to my physical needs, your phone call was my only typical interruption. If 7:30 arrived and I did not hear from you, I was quick to call. How novel and odd life is for me since I cannot reach you on the other end of the phone.

I am again in the practice of fidgeting in my bed in the early mornings, as I did when you first passed. I roll from side to side then spread out on my belly, only to repeat the poses, right side, left side, and belly down. I am like the mini sausages a chef prepares on the grill, a few minutes of heat on each side, a quick slice and then compressed; my subliminal sausage dance.

It is not the same rude reminder of your death as last year. I am not wakening with my hair soaked in a puddle of my hot tears, coupled with the sensation of blazing pokers prodding my body. I think I do the subliminal sausage dance each morning, as it is a full calendar year since your passing. I still cry at times, the tears no longer scalding. Instead, they fall like warm rain, uncontrollable yet welcomed for short periods.

Over and Out For Now

Love Joie

#52. Study Questions

Food for Thought

1. Describe what you consider to be a celestial visit?

2. Describe how people silently commune with each other.

Matters of the Heart

1. Discuss the essence and energy of love, considering:
   (a) does the essence and energy of love ever die?
   (b) in what ways do we continue to experience the essence and energy of a loved one even after they die?
   (c) have you known the essence and energy of love to present itself in dreams? Please elaborate.

Joie loves
to
hear from her readers

✉ j@readred.ca

🐦 @readjread

📷 @joieread

f @joieread

Made in the USA
Columbia, SC
21 September 2018